CHANGE WITH CONFIDENCE

CHANGE WITH CONFIDENCE

Answers to the 50 Biggest
Questions that Keep
Change Leaders Up at Night

By Phil Buckley

JJ JOSSEY-BASS™
A Wiley Brand

Published by Jossey-Bass
A Wiley Imprint
Published simultaneously in the United States of America and Canada.
www.josseybass.com

National Library of Canada Cataloguing in Publication Data

Buckley, Phil
   Change with confidence : answers to the 50 biggest questions that keep change leaders up at night / Phil Buckley.
Includes index.
Issued also in electronic formats.
ISBN 978-1-118-55655-9
   1. Organizational change.   2. Leadership.   I. Title.
HD58.8.B83 2013   658.4'06   C2013-900607-9
ISBN: 978-1-118-55658-0 (ebk); 978-1-118-55656-6 (ebk); 978-1-118-55657-3 (ebk)

Production Credits
Cover design: Adrian So
Typesetting: Laserwords
Cover photograph: © Photomorphic / iStockphoto
Printer: Friesens

Editorial Credits
Executive editor: Karen Milner
Managing editor: Alison Maclean
Production editor: Pamela Vokey

John Wiley & Sons Canada, Limited.
6045 Freemont Blvd.
Mississauga, Ontario
L5R 4J3

Printed in Canada

1 2 3 4 5 FP 17 16 15 14 13

To Barb, Sam, and Charlie, the brightest lights of my life.

CONTENTS

PREFACE

MY FIRST CORPORATE ROLE was at the Business Development Bank of Canada (BDC) selling and delivering training programs to small and medium-sized businesses. This Crown corporation didn't have the marketing funds that its competitors had, and this hurt its ability to grow. The organization consisted of a network of 77 offices across Canada that sold services to different geographic areas. The training managers from three nearby offices and I formed a partnership and pooled our funds so we could compete for larger contracts. The strategy worked and sales grew.

As our confidence increased we started going after contracts that had been exclusively tendered to Canada's top six consulting firms. Sales grew further. Word of our success spread and within the bank we became known as "Miami Vice" because we were the new kids on the block, did things differently, and spent most of our paychecks on clothes. We wrote a report on our newfound success and proposed that BDC restructure its independent branches into larger "super-branches" that would offer all financial and consulting services. Our district manager didn't like the idea and told us it wouldn't work. We were convinced it would and that we had invented the "future of banking." We shared our idea with the regional boss (our district manager's boss), and he loved it. Within two years, the first super-branch was opened in downtown Toronto. At the launch ceremony the regional manager said, "You know, if it hadn't been for you guys, this wouldn't have happened." We were proud.

Business is one of the largest forces that impacts our lives, whether through the products sold and services offered or the working environments provided, and when companies are in flux, so too are their employees. While it may appear otherwise, most companies are in constant flux. Economic globalization has intensified the need for businesses to continually adapt and reinvent themselves in order to stay competitive and improve their performance. Most need to rethink and change the way they operate or suffer the consequences of poor performance, or, worse, become irrelevant. Constant change is a business reality, and the people who make the wheels turn must constantly change what they do and how they do it.

People rarely choose to be on a project involving a big organizational change; they are chosen, and, once briefed by their bosses, their work and personal lives immediately change. Meeting requests flood their email inboxes, and many people they don't know want to meet with them; their to-do lists overflow, and the time available to accomplish tasks seems to evaporate. This is so often true whether someone is an executive sponsor (who funds and has overall accountability for projects), a project manager (who runs the day-to-day operations), or a team member (who has a project-specific role). For all change leaders, life becomes uncertain, often threatening. When they need the most confidence, many have the least to guide them.

The first big change project I led started the same way. My meeting schedule devoured my days (and nights); everyone was in "action mode," with little time to brief me; and there was no downtime to figure out what I needed to do or how to do it. People assumed I had been chosen to lead the project because I had done it before and knew what I was doing—I hadn't and I didn't—which made me even more anxious. Survival became my main objective: How was I going to pull this off and be a leader? Years later, I learned that many change leaders, from supervisors to CEOs, had similar experiences, and, like me, soldiered through their doubts and concerns, doing their best and learning through their mistakes (some more costly than others).

At the BDC, I learned a lot about how people change. Building capabilities for many types of businesses (and people) taught me that the mechanics of organizational change were the same regardless of whether I was working at a steel mill or an accounting firm—change principles are universal. I also realized that change is all about people and whether they choose to change or not.

My next role was at Sales Performance Group, a boutique consulting firm that redesigned sales and marketing organizations. Each company we worked with felt that its culture was unique—and it was, which required us to customize approaches to earn trust and support before we could help improve the business. Cultural pride is a powerful positive force unless it causes people to explain away poor performance or hold onto old ways of working that no longer benefit the business. Ingrained behaviors can be the silent assassins of change.

From there, I moved to Cadbury, a company constantly changing to meet (and even exceed) consumer, customer, and shareholder expectations. It was a big player in the confectionery business but a small one in the food business, and there was always a wolf at the door to ward off or a dragon to slay to be successful. At all times at least one big change was in play—restructures, efficiency drives, mergers, demergers, operating model redesigns, new systems—that was transforming the organization, and this made life there vibrant, exciting, and, yes, full of anxiety.

I witnessed the power of a humanistic approach to change management when we adopted the Value Based Management philosophy in 2000. Sir John Sunderland, Cadbury's chief executive officer, described it as "not just about financial management. It is 20 percent about the numbers and 80 percent about the people and culture, because people create value."[1] This may seem like simple common sense, but so few organizations realize that *people* make big changes successful, and a change project team's role is therefore to provide them with what they need to do it well. Treating people with respect and dignity as they take on changes pays.

In my experience, the people-first approach succeeded in 27 big change projects across 22 countries, and when Kraft Foods bought Cadbury for $19.6 billion in February 2010, I was selected to co-lead the global integration with an excellent change leader from Kraft. Our collaborative and inclusive approach to integrating the two businesses worked well with the 20 leadership teams that we partnered with.

Many change leaders don't realize that the people who must adopt the changes are the ones who control the long-term success of the project, and if they don't take on new ways of working (and stick with them), the project will ultimately fail and most benefits will be lost. Therefore, the best strategy for ensuring success is to work *with* people and make sure they have everything they need—including respect, encouragement, information, tools, and the opportunity to shape the change to fit their environment. Positive change happens and is sustainable when it is organic, when it grows from the bottom up.

The opposite approach, top-down and dictatorial, is disastrous. If you don't respect people, they won't respect the change (and little will change). If you don't earn trust, you won't get accurate information. If training isn't sufficient, people will make errors (and go back to the work habits they know). If they don't participate in designing the change and how it is implemented, they won't be engaged or committed. Finally, if leaders don't change first, the people actually being asked to do the heavy lifting won't either. I have seen change leaders attempt to force changes through fear and threats. This might work in the short run but always fails over time. A forced change loses its steam as soon as the pressure is removed.

Confidence plays an important role in leading a big change project. It improves your focus and galvanizes your resolve to make good decisions around the questions that are critical to the project's (and your) success.

I wrote this book to help leaders build their confidence by applying practical, people-focused advice and approaches to working through a big change project. Although every change has its own circumstances, there are proven processes, tactics, and behaviors that support those going through change that lead to sustainable success.

The book is structured around 50 questions I was asked time and time again. They are all excellent questions, and to manage change successfully you need to be able to answer them, and to answer them well. Many who haven't dealt with these questions before either proceed based on the first information they receive or rely on their gut instincts. Unbeknownst to them, they send the team charging down a path full of potential land mines.

The best support I can give you, change leader, is to disavow high theorizing and take practical, experience-based advice on how to answer key questions.

Since most change leaders have little time to read books on how to lead a change project well, I have created a resource that can be dipped into as needed. (Of course, I would love it if you read it from cover to cover.) Each chapter provides information on answering an important question about a big change project. The layout is simple, for easy navigation and quick access to the information you need. First, an opening quotation provides context for and insight on the question being explored. Most of the quotations are from people outside the business world, which underscores a key theme that change is about people, all kinds of people, and that business has a lot to learn from them. Next, I provide insights on why you need to consider the question and how doing so will help you be successful (and avoid setbacks). Two case studies demonstrate good and poor practices regarding the topic, half of them drawn from my personal experience on big change projects, the other half from private and public organizations around the world. A list of effective practices gives you practical advice on how to manage critical aspects of big changes. Finally, a template provides an example that illustrates the information you will need to capture.

All big change projects require significant adjustments to current ways of doing things. Most require new attitudes and capabilities, new or altered processes and systems, and new work relationships. Perseverance is also essential to embed changes so that they stick long term. This book will help you make big change projects successful, enhance your career, and retain your sanity. Your change project could be the biggest and most exciting opportunity in your career, and my goal is to help set you up for success.

How to Use This Book

I have found that the most useful business books are the ones easiest to navigate. The structure and content are organized in a way that helps me find information I need. This was my goal as I formatted this book: to make it easy for you to dip in and out of based on what you need.

Structure

The book spans all aspects of a big change project, from when an organization initiates a big change to when the project team hands over responsibility to the organization's operating teams. It is divided into four sections, one for each phase of a change project. I call these "Figuring It Out," "Planning for Change," "Managing Change," and "Making Change Stick." This framework will help you find information based on where you are in a project.

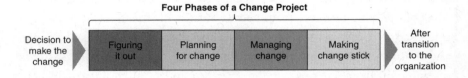

Figuring It Out: How to get your head around what you have been asked to do.

Planning for Change: How to create a plan that outlines what needs to happen, by when, and by whom.

Managing Change: How to maintain momentum as you manage the dynamics of the project.

Making Change Stick: Embedding the change into regular operations.

Though change management is rarely linear, describing it using a start-to-finish approach will show you how the types of questions change throughout a project.

Content

I've observed that change leaders need the most support when facing questions they don't know how to answer. Therefore, this book is organized around the key questions common to big change projects. All of them were raised repeatedly during projects I worked on. They relate to both the project management and people dynamics aspects of change. The human elements are the most challenging because they require adjustments to the current organization's culture, the collective behaviors that define how people treat one another and how they get things done. They are also the most important because people make change, and if you don't help people manage their personal lives, they won't successfully manage the business change. Change is about people, a truth often forgotten by change leaders.

Each question is a chapter of the book, and within each chapter I provide the following:

- Context around the significance of the question and why it needs to be considered.
- Stories that illustrate good (👍) and bad (👎) practices
- Specific actions that help you answer the questions

The quotations opening each chapter help illustrate what lies at the heart of each question. For 14 years I distributed a weekly digest of business articles that always included a well-known quotation. I realized the power of these quotations when readers sent me notes about the clarity they provided. The ones selected for this book reflect my views on change based on my experience. Many come from outstanding people outside the business world, and most are humanist in nature, underscoring my belief that to successfully manage a business change you *must* successfully manage people through change.

Another recurring feature of the book is working templates that provide a starting point for making balanced decisions. They summarize the data you need to identify and choose the best options—facts, options, and rationale—and each contains an example with sample data from a project I managed. URL addresses are provided so that you can download blank templates to use on your change projects.

Perhaps the best advice on how to use this book is to reference it when you face something you don't know how to do. Pick it up and look through the table of contents for the area where you need perspective or to consider things further, or to find specific options for solving a problem.

PART 1

Figuring It Out

ALL CHANGE PROJECTS REQUIRE you to move people from how they currently think and act to new ways of thinking and acting. The underlying rationale for change must be that it will lead to better performance, but this starting point is rarely enough for people to make them change. They are usually set in their ways and need to be constantly motivated and supported in order to take on new ways of working. Inertia is a human, perhaps all-too-human, part of our DNA, and this needs to be acknowledged before it can be overcome.

There are many factors to consider as you assess the scope and magnitude of your change project. Often, change leaders make commitments regarding a big organizational change before doing their homework. They don't spend enough time understanding where colleagues currently are and where they need to be. Comparing these two positions will give you a sense of what needs to change (mind-sets, behaviors, skills, processes, and systems), how big of a change is required, and how difficult it will be to make. In total, assessing all of these aspects of your change project will give you a sense of exactly what you have been asked to do.

The Plan

CHAPTER 1

What Do I Bring to the Project?

Begin with your strengths.
—**Azim Premji**

OFTEN, PEOPLE BECOME PARALYZED by the magnitude of a big change project regardless of the role they've been given, be it executive sponsor, project manager, or project team member. They compare the project goals with the status quo, become anxious, and allow comments like "We've never done this before" or "If we don't do this, we won't reach our annual financial goals" to fuel doubt, fear, and panic. Before this happens, think of what you can draw upon to help the organization make the change. You were chosen for your role because you have skills beyond the obvious ones that connect you to the project (e.g., being a manager in a Finance department undergoing restructuring). Based on your initial briefing, what past experiences, knowledge, skills, and relationships are relevant to the project? Taking stock of what makes you the best person for the job will focus your energy and build confidence. You may be surprised by how much you have to offer and how these abilities will benefit you over the course of the project.

Thumbs Down, Thumbs Up

In 2005, the Swedish Road Administration (SRoA) and County Administrative Boards (CoAs) initiated an e-service project to automate probationary driver's license applications. The two government agencies were responsible for different steps in the process, which citizens found confusing. The project provided the opportunity to standardize processes across the nation's 21 county offices, and automating it through one website was deemed a good solution.

The project manager had no public e-service experience and very limited IT knowledge. He also did not have many contacts within the 21 county offices, making it difficult for him to facilitate consensus on common criteria for judging applications. As well, he had difficulty convincing office managers to follow the proposed launch schedule, and this slowed down the transition process. The project was completed in 2007, a full year after its original deadline.

In 2009, Merck & Company acquired Schering-Plough Corporation for $41 billion and became the world's second-largest pharmaceutical company. The Merck & Company CEO appointed his head of global marketing to lead the integration. The new project leader said, "I remember going home that night and taking out a blank sheet of paper and saying, 'What do I do tomorrow?'" [1] He reviewed his network and reached out to peers who could guide him in areas he was less familiar with (e.g., supply chain, research and development, regulatory, etc.), including contacts at Schering-Plough, with whom he was involved in a joint venture in 2004. He also hired specialist consultants to coach him on aspects of the merger in which neither he nor his team had any direct experience. The merger was successful, with 16 of 20 top markets integrating within six months and 8 of the top 10 products growing through this period. He was soon promoted to a more senior position as president of Merck's global human health business.

What Works

- Note the colleagues you know in the areas of the business experiencing the change. They will give you insider perspectives on needs, concerns, and cultural norms.

- Think of what you have in common with the impacted groups. Personal credibility and trust is important when supporting teams through change.

- Review what projects you have worked on and what you learned from them.

- Read past performance appraisals and record the skills and capabilities you have been recognized for. Ask peers to add to your list.

- Think of the project managers you have worked with and what skills and behaviors they demonstrated. Which ones contributed to (and detracted from) their performance? Why? Meet with these project managers to get their views on what worked and didn't work.

Identifying the unique experiences, skills, and behaviors you bring to the project is the best way to start building a plan to successfully manage your role. Draw upon these assets as you develop a deeper understanding of your project (and what has to be done to make it successful).

CHAPTER 2

How Do I Identify What Needs to Change?

If you want to change attitudes, start with a
change in behavior.
—**Katharine Hepburn**

ANY BIG CHANGE WILL AFFECT HOW PEOPLE do their work, encompassing their attitudes, behaviors, processes, roles, the people they interact with, and the software they use. A critical initial step is to thoroughly map out what needs to be different for the change to be successful. This will give you a sense of how difficult your change project will be for individuals and teams to adopt.

Status quo work environments have nuanced codes of conduct that often go unnoticed unless you dig deeply to find them, and eliminating some of these ways of working can be as important as starting new ones. It's critical not to underestimate the changes required. Your assessment will directly affect the resources needed to implement change, and misestimating the resources required will lead either to a mid-project request for additional funds (not pleasant) or an understaffed implementation (not wise). Moreover, missed requirements will distract and frustrate your team because they come as a surprise, and might put in question the quality of your plan, or, even worse, your leadership.

Thumbs Down, Thumbs Up

👎 The Canada Firearms Registry was established by the federal government as a response to a wave of gun-related crimes in urban centers across the country. In 1996, the Canada Firearms Centre was created to oversee the administration of the registry. Its mandate was the mandatory licensing of gun owners and the registration of all firearms by 2003. The stakeholders most impacted by the legislation weren't sufficiently consulted, and this resulted in a backlash from many farmers, hunters, and members of gun lobby groups, who attempted to sabotage the new registry and legislation.

The project plan did not anticipate the number of design changes needed to existing databases or the changes to processes and software upgrades to federal and provincial departments connected to it. Also, it did not account for the skills required to fill out the registration form, resulting in a high level of error. Ninety percent of the submitted forms required follow-up, and the agency staff had to be expanded from a handful to 600.

The success of the registry itself is debatable, but the success in implementing it is not. A large system project predicted to cost taxpayers $2 million (after registry fees) ballooned to $1 billion—a 50,000 percent cost overrun. On November 1, 2012, it was announced that all data held within the registry, other than from Quebec, had been destroyed.

👍 When Kraft Foods acquired Cadbury, a project team was set up to create a new innovation process, with members from both companies and all regions invited to join. As the new process developed, team members provided feedback from their business areas, and discussed all ideas raised. The final version of the innovation process included the best elements of both legacy processes. It was shared with the regional leadership teams to ensure that no perspectives had been missed before it went to the global leadership team for approval. The project leader understood that all groups working with current processes were needed to define the change and make it successful.

What Works

- Identify the attitude and mind-set changes first—they are often the hardest to identify, most difficult to address, and take the longest time to implement.

- Focus on detailing the behaviors that need to change for each level and department. Behavior changes are the most visible signals that new ways of working are taking hold, and they can generate tremendous momentum.

- Assign a "high," "medium," or "low" rating for each change, to determine which changes require the most adjustments and which groups will be most heavily affected.

- Engage people early in the assessment process so that they feel part of the initiative and take ownership of the change process—colleague inclusion and participation is essential for successful change projects.

- Test your evolving hypotheses with leadership team members. Their reactions will help you connect the dots and create an overall storyline.

- Review skill gaps, which can be contentious, with department leaders to ensure that they are dealt with. "From" and "to" charts (see below) are helpful because they provide visual representations of gaps—for example, selling skills.

Capability Gap Analysis

From	To	Capability Gap
Selling individual product promotions to achieve a defined volume target	Selling a cluster of different product promotions with volume and profitability targets	Commercial math, analysis, forecasting

*http://www.changewithconfidence.com/?page_id=69

- In addition to department changes, document and assign people resources based on changes that affect multiple departments—for example, a forecasting process that receives inputs from Sales, Marketing, and Manufacturing. This area of transition is often ignored or is considered a secondary concern because most organizations structure themselves around individual departments. But multiple departments providing input on new processes will reveal requirements on how information needs to flow across the business, and this will determine when handoffs between parties need to occur.

- Make sure someone is accountable for each aspect of the change project. Any unaccounted-for areas either will not be attended to or will be seen as extra work by those who eventually have to handle them.

- Chart the required changes by groups responsible for them. This is an effective way of understanding the magnitude of the overall change. Describe the current and future states in terms of the mind-sets, behaviors, processes, and systems that need to change. Assign high, medium, and low levels of difficulty and any interdependencies with other teams. Most important impacts tend to be mind-sets—for example, Sales and Marketing need to see themselves as equal partners in managing customer promotions.

- Ensure that someone from the project team participates in every department or work-team impact assessment. This ensures a consistent approach is used and avoids confusion, missed requirements, and having to rework certain assignments.

You will have a sense of the size of the project once the assessment is completed. The number and magnitude of changes will provide a top-line view of the project's scope, and you can further refine the requirements by studying similar projects that have been managed in the past. Organizations all manage change differently, and their histories will provide clues for success in the present.

Impact Assessment*

Impacted Group	Current State	Future State	Transition State (if applicable)	Mind-Set/ Attitude	Behavior	Process	System	Interdependency with Other Teams
Sales	Forecast provided on day eight of the month	Forecast provided on day six of the month	Trial test for one month	H: Confidence in making estimates with less data	H: Greater reliance on in-field data	M: Adjustments to models and calendar	L: Minor adjustment to timing prompts	H: Marketing, Supply Chain, Finance

*Level of difficulty: H = high, M = medium, L = low.

**http://www.changewithconfidence.com/?page_id=71

CHAPTER 3

What Have We Done Before, and Did It Work?

Those who don't know history are destined to repeat it.
—Edmund Burke

REVIEWING LESSONS LEARNED from big change projects is the fastest way to anticipate how the organization will perceive your project. People create meaning from past experiences, and these experiences are key to knowing how you can positively position your project. This information is held by colleagues who led or worked on the projects, and by overlaying the details of your project with those from the past you will see clearly those aspects likely to be supported and those that aren't. Highlighting past successes and incorporating answers to likely objections will help you form positive first impressions. Failing to gather and use this information ignores the collective wisdom of the very people you need to create positive change.

Often, new change leaders believe their project will be more successful than past big change initiatives without identifying why. If most of your company's change projects have been unsuccessful, you must ask yourself what will be different about your project.

Thumbs Down, Thumbs Up

At Cadbury Adams Canada, a commercial team decided to harmonize the packaging of a group of different products so that when merchandized together they formed a visual block of color, helping them stand out on the shelf against their competitors. The team reasoned that the more the products stood out, the better they would sell.

The strategy failed largely because many retailers bought only the popular chocolate bars, making the strong visual impact on the shelves impossible to achieve. Also, some consumers found it difficult to recognize their favorite brand with the new packaging and therefore chose a recognizable competitive chocolate bar instead. The strategy was dropped.

Seven years later, in 2005, a new commercial team decided to employ the same strategy. The project went ahead even though sales colleagues with years of experience cautioned against doing so because of the results of the first initiative. After initial launch distribution gains and promotions, sales began to fall. In less than two years, the commercial team brought back the original "classic" packaging. Sales colleagues were overheard saying "I knew it" and "I told you so." The new team was not successful because it did not make its strategy significantly better and different from that which had failed in the past.

In 2011, Southern Seawater Desalination Plant (SSDP) began operations as the largest water treatment plant in the southern and eastern hemispheres. A new source of drinking water was essential for Perth, Australia, because natural water inflows into the local dam system had decreased by over 70 percent since 1974. The project team needed to complete planning, approvals, and procurement processes within two years, less than half the time demanded of similar projects. The team was able to shorten the project time by three years by using lessons learned from the building of a similar facility the previous year. A lot of the data generated from the neighboring Perth Seawater Desalination Plant plan was built into the business case, and this saved considerable time, a necessity given the strict requirements for verified feasibility studies and environmental consultancy. The new plant adopted the same procurement method, including criteria for supplier selection—expertise in process design, reverse osmosis technology, and energy optimization. Furthermore, partnership relations benefited from an in-depth understanding of risk allocation and local community consultations used by the first plant. The SSDP was opened on time and quickly received approval for doubling capacity.

What Works

- Interview as many people as possible to get as many diverse perspectives as you can on past projects, and look for positive threads across these views.

- Spend time seeking out long-term colleagues who can offer details about why projects in the past worked or didn't.

- Ask very specific questions about other big change initiatives implemented in the last five years, including:

  - How many were completed and how many shelved?

  - Were the leadership teams honest about the projects' purposes and outcomes?

  - How many projects were viewed as successful?

  - How many had sustained leadership support?

  - What worked and didn't work? Why?

  - How many resulted in colleagues losing something they valued?

- Review all written documentation on past change projects (keeping in mind that projects that didn't go well tend to be less well documented and analyzed).

- If similar projects have failed in the past, explain why your project is different and how it will be successful.

- Create an organization interview guide to help you stay focused. Such a template will allow you to uncover commonalities, differences, and trends among the responses you receive.

The environment in which your change project operates will be influenced by past successes and failures. Understanding what has worked and what didn't will allow you to position your project in a favorable light.

Organization Interview Guide

Question	Initiative 1	Initiative 2	Initiative 3
Was the project successful?	Yes	Yes	No
Did it have a good leadership sponsor?	Yes—Marketing head	No—midlevel manager–led	No—initial support by leadership team but no one owned it
What worked?	− Training was aligned with needs— codeveloped with Marketing	− Communications and colleague participation	
What didn't work?		− Executive support to remove barriers − Poor attendance at training sessions necessitating additional catch-up sessions	− Training could have been better—no participation from management − Communication of project benefits
What did colleagues gain and lose?	+ Better tools − Less local direction on strategy	+ Greater local decision making − More complex processes	− Less effective communications across business − Longer and more demanding approval processes

*http://www.changewithconfidence.com/?page_id=75

CHAPTER 4

What Other Change Projects Are Going On?

Everything is connected.

—Paul Hawken

YOUR ORGANIZATION'S BUSINESS ENVIRONMENT will have a direct impact on the success of your project, and current performance and leadership interests will influence resourcing and executive attention. One critical factor in your project's success is the amount of change going on when you implement the project. People have limited capacity for change and the extra work that comes with change projects. Generally, the more change initiatives in play, the more challenges a project has to overcome, and each other initiative can derail your project as it draws on limited resources and takes up executives' time.

A business environment assessment analyzing the company's activities will tell you what other projects are active and what demands have already been placed on colleagues. This will answer the question, "Can these teams handle my project on top of everything else that is going on?" by way of answering, "What changes are being made to ways of working?", "Are these changes aligned with yours?", "Who is working on these projects?", and "Are they the same people you need for your project?" A delay in another project's timeline could delay your project, and this information will better allow you to plan the timing of your project and build in contingencies.

Thumbs Down, Thumbs Up

In 2003, DHL, a global leader in the logistics industry, greatly expanded its North American presence by acquiring Airborne Express in the United States and Mayne Logistics Loomis in Canada. Overnight it became the number three player in both markets, after FedEx and UPS. The $1.2-billion expansion included seven new U.S. regional sorting centers, as well as upgrading 12 distribution hubs and the company's IT infrastructure. However, there was no overall vision for the expansion or plan to connect the various change projects, and each was run independently with no information sharing between them. Since organization structures and roles had not been finalized—including issues such as which employees were being retained—it was difficult to engage the business teams, and it was unclear how to manage cross-project conflicts. Since the different company cultures had not been integrated, old power structures slowed progress and impeded communications. In the end, the new e-procurement software solution did not work, resulting in widespread customer service problems. In 2008, DHL announced it was exiting the U.S. domestic market, after incurring a $10-billion loss over five years.

In 2004, Cadbury Adams USA harmonized its enterprise operating system, a major project requiring significant resources. When certain milestones were in danger of being missed, the project team discovered that key people were not living up to their time commitments. Further investigation revealed that most of them had been assigned to projects totaling over 150 percent of their available time. (One unlucky soul was 200 percent allocated. He always looked tired.) It was impossible for them to honor their commitments. Certain projects were reprioritized, reducing commitments for these colleagues, and additional resources were added where this was not possible. Further delays were avoided by ensuring that sufficient resources were made available to manage the work. Insufficient resources is one of the biggest causes of project failure.

What Works

- Survey all departments to see what changes are taking place, how big they are, what the key communication messages need to be, and what team members have to do.
- Create a business environment assessment template to identify the commitments of other change initiatives on colleagues affected by your change project. Highlight overlapping projects and any interdependencies across projects.

Business Environment Assessment

Question	Project 1	Project 2	Project 3
What changes are being made to ways of working?	Stronger process for expense approval and metrics	Collaborative culture	Greater focus on fact-based decision making
Are these changes aligned with yours?	No—a more detailed process may conflict with process simplification initiative	Yes	Yes
What resource commitments have been made?	See Resource Allocation Summary	See Resource Allocation Summary	See Resource Allocation Summary
Does this limit the amount of resources for your project? How?	Yes	No	No
Are there any interdependencies with your project? What are they?	Yes—these changes must be made before switching to new procedures	No	No

*http://www.changewithconfidence.com/?page_id=79

- Identify synergies among projects. Do they share team members? Are they trying to achieve the same outcomes? Could some of the work be incorporated within another project? Does the capacity exist to start your project at this time? If not, what needs to change to do so?

- Develop "go now" and "delay" options, and include pros and cons of each.

- Share your analysis with the leadership team to get its perspective on the level of "change traffic" across the organization.

- Track resource commitments for all active projects. Typically, some resources are assigned more project and operational responsibilities than the time available to complete them. This is powerful data to share with leadership teams and managers of resources, and it should ensure that you get sufficient support.

Resource Allocation Summary

Name	Level	Project 1	Project 2	Project 3	Total Commitment
John	Director	10% of time commitment		20%	30%
Raj	Senior Manager	50%	10%	50%	110%
Sarah	Analyst	50%		15%	

http://www.changewithconfidence.com/?page_id=81

Often, change leaders assume that their project is the only game in town. Usually, however, there are multiple change projects competing for limited resources that make the work of the people you need to take on the change more complex. Managing your project with a solid understanding of the business environment will allow you to be realistic about the commitments and resources you have to achieve your goals. Once you have a good understanding of the operating environment, you can focus on the people who directly impact your project, the stakeholders.

Communication

CHAPTER 5

Who Are the Stakeholders Who Can Influence Success?

When you want culture to change you have to put yourself into the shoes of the stakeholders.
—Esther Cameron and Mike Green

STAKEHOLDERS CAN EITHER HELP OR HINDER your project, and thus stakeholder management is critical to successful change projects. Stakeholders are individuals or groups that are either impacted by the change or have influence over the direction (and evaluation) of the project. Leaders of the organization are important stakeholders and you need to engage and motivate these key players by understanding what their needs and concerns are. They can give you access to resources, complete tasks, make connections, and, perhaps most importantly, drive cultural change by aligning their behavior with the new ways of working. If you lobby stakeholders effectively, they will remove barriers to your plan and encourage people to adopt the changes you need. External stakeholders—customers, consumers, suppliers, government, and the community—are as important as internal ones.

Thumbs Down, Thumbs Up

In 2004, Qantas, Australia's national airline, moved to a new parts management system called Jetsmart and did so without getting any input from the engineers (licensed airplane mechanics) who would be using it. The employees' union claimed the software was difficult to use and unnecessarily increased the engineers' workload. Qantas's chief financial officer told *Australian IT Magazine*, "We wouldn't ask the engineers what their views on our software systems were. We'll put in what we think is appropriate for us." The union responded by advising its members not to assist with the implementation of the system aircraft engineers referred to as "Dumbjet." In 2008, Qantas announced it was replacing the $40 million Jetsmart software.

👍 In 2004, Marriott International embarked on a two-year, $90 million Bedding Program to upgrade the bedding at 2,400 hotels across 10 lodging brands in 68 countries. The stakeholder group was vast and included consumers, who provided the rationale for the program and evaluated the new bedding; owners and franchisees, who paid for the program; housekeepers and laundry associates, who needed to maintain the new standards with new linens; property management teams, which ordered the new items; local governments, which had local regulations; suppliers (of over 1,850 new types of products); a global procurement team, which negotiated all supplier contracts; and 21 internal project teams, with 200 employees in total. The project manager engaged all stakeholder groups and facilitated communications between them. The project was a huge success and came in on time and under budget.

What Works

- Get an executive sponsor—the more senior and highly regarded, the better.
- Interview all key stakeholders, to understand how the project fits with their agendas. What do they stand to gain and lose from the change, and how interested are they in seeing the project succeed?
- Ask questions about their perceptions of the project:
  - What have you heard about the project?
  - What hurdles need to be overcome?

- What is important to keep top-of-mind as we progress? (These are usually personal needs or fears.)

- What does success look like to you?

- What will indicate that the project has been successful? (This will tell you what measurements are meaningful to stakeholders.)

• Document your interviews on a stakeholder analysis template (see chart on the next page). It is important to know how each stakeholder will be affected by the change, that stakeholder's current level of interest and support, how aligned this is with your requirements of that stakeholder, and what you need to do to close any gaps. Short one-on-one interviews are usually sufficient to understand these details.

Stakeholder relationships must be two-way streets: the stakeholders need your coaching to honor their commitments, and you need their support. By understanding what is important to each of your key stakeholders, you can make your project more meaningful to them and gain their trust and participation. A happy stakeholder is a supportive stakeholder.

Key stakeholder support is necessary but not sufficient to make a big change successful. You also need the support of everyone who is affected by the new ways of working. Knowing what people are informally saying among themselves about your change will give you a good indication of what attitudes you are starting with.

Stakeholder Analysis

Stakeholders in New Innovation Process	How Will They Benefit?	How Will They Lose?	What Support Do I Need from Them?	How Motivated Are They about the Project?	What Actions Do I Need to Take to Maximize Benefits?	By When?
Marketing Director	• Less rework • More new product projects	• Slower decision making across departments	• Sponsor process changes • Communications to organization	• Very supportive	• Develop strong guiding principles • Drive project with speed	January
	• Greater department participation					June
Sales Director	• Earlier input into product decisions		• Communications to Sales team	• Neutral	• Reinforce customer benefits of better product launch execution versus current service gap	January
Supply Chain Director	• Greater visibility of new product development		• Communications to Supply Chain	• Supportive	• Reinforce production efficiencies	January

CHAPTER 6

What Is the Water Cooler Talk about Your Proposed Change?

Rumors are like ripples in a cornfield. They are ephemeral,
but they do indicate which way the wind is blowing.

—Susan J. Palmer

"WATER COOLER TALK" IS A GREAT METAPHOR for what colleagues think and say when not pressured to toe the company line, and understanding such uncensored beliefs will enable you to amplify positive perceptions and refute negative ones. Shaped by past experiences, beliefs are part of your organization's culture. They are expressed through hero and horror stories alike, and while positive stories lead to greater receptivity to new projects, horror stories lead to apprehension.

Numerous companies fall into the pattern of starting many initiatives but successfully completing only a few. Colleagues become accustomed to strong project launches with lots of fanfare and then little follow-through—some projects even seem to disappear. Without proper communications and leadership support, once an initiative is launched, people will already be looking for the "next big thing," and you won't get the kind of sustained engagement you need.

Addressing colleague concerns in project communications will increase the credibility of your project and the level of trust in the project team. Furthermore, differences between "water cooler" exchanges and executive interviews will help you assess how in touch leaders are with the feelings of their team members and what views may need reconciling before the project gets underway.

Thumbs Down, Thumbs Up

In 2004, Aventis Pharma, a German-owned, South Africa–based pharmaceutical company, was bought by Sanofi-Synthélabo, a French-owned South African competitor. Aventis Pharma's culture was bottom-up, with local leaders making most decisions, whereas Sanofi-Synthélabo's culture was top-down, with most decisions being made by executives in Paris. A new local leadership team was created, and most positions went to Sanofi-Synthélabo staff. Since there was no merger project team, there was little communication on business integration changes. Managerial staff attended only one briefing when the sale was announced, and manufacturing staff didn't receive any communication at all. As changes (staff reductions, new global processes and procedures, and new cost savings goals) were implemented, rumors circulated about their manufacturing plant being closed. Each new way of working was seen as a plot against workers. Many believed that if they questioned any change, they would be fired.

The Aventis employees' union, which had previously been treated as an equal partner in making all process changes, was now a reluctant recipient of foreign head office changes. Rumors began that the new company was intentionally trying to frustrate workers; workers, for their part, started talking about the union being weak, as it could no longer challenge company decisions. In 2007, an employee survey revealed that 28 percent of manufacturing employees still did not know why changes were being made, 67 percent felt that the merger had negatively impacted their morale, and 64 percent said they would leave the company if given the opportunity.

In 1993, Neilson Cadbury Canada entered the export market through a partnership with Sabritas, a division of PepsiCo International, to produce and distribute chocolate bars in Mexico. Shaquille O'Neal was the celebrity who endorsed the candy bar, and his smiling face was on the wrapper. Initial sales went through the roof, and manufacturing capacity became an issue. Moving to a 24/7 production schedule was not permitted under union contracts. The operators, however, often talked about the rising demand for their work and were proud of their product's international success. Some even talked about the new requirements being a sign of job security, backed up by a raise for those who adopted the new schedule. A vote was held and the colleagues overwhelmingly opted for the new schedule. Since the change was regarded as positive, it was easier to get agreement on changes to existing labor agreements.

What Works

- Informally poll colleagues to get an accurate picture of how they feel about the ways of working you intend to change.
- Get communications out early on the benefits of your project.
- Ensure you have input from every group impacted by the change.
- Thank people for providing their concerns. Validating and addressing them in an open way builds trust.
- Quickly dispel any incorrect information, identify areas where there are negative reactions to the change, and provide ongoing opportunities for people to raise concerns.

Colleague Interview Guide

Theme	Area 1	Area 2	Area 3
"Every project results in more work for everyone."		"This project means more time away for training."	"I just got used to the last change that was made six months ago."
"Our company changes to get better."	"I remember when we changed our sales structure. It made us a player in the market."		"Our president is always open to new ways of working, like last year when he authorized a new computer system."

*http://www.changewithconfidence.com/?page_id=89

- Create a colleague interview guide to help you gather information quickly. Record comments verbatim to reveal the levels of emotion behind views, and select one that best describes a specific theme.

Knowing how colleagues feel about your proposed change gives you rich information on what current attitudes will support and hinder your project. It also gives you a reading on how important the change is to them and how difficult it might be to implement. This information is critical to your overall assessment of what can be realistically delivered.

Getting Results

CHAPTER 7

What Do I Need to Know Before I Commit to Deliverables?

Don't set people up for failure by promising that you will deliver high levels of output . . . Everyone loses when such ambitious targets are missed: you look bad, people's self-confidence falls even further, and your superiors are upset.
—William Bridges

Beware the time-driven project with an artificial deadline.
—M. Dobson

BIG CHANGE PROJECTS ARE RARELY managed in perfect conditions. You need to ensure that the expectations of the various team leaders are aligned with the conditions surrounding the project by weighing the deliverables against the level of change involved, resource availability, and the environment in which the impacted colleagues are working. Think of this assessment as a test where you start with a perfect score and marks are subtracted or added based on circumstances that hinder or support the change. A mark is subtracted if colleagues believe there is a hidden agenda behind the change and a mark awarded if the leadership team agrees to all obligations requested by the project team. In real life, not all pluses and minuses are equal. This mental image, however, can be a quick way to take stock of your situation.

First, determine how big the change will be for colleagues. Does it represent a minor modification or a significant change in mind-set that challenges what made them successful in the past? Implementing a big change adds stress to an organization. Colleagues usually take on the responsibilities of people sequestered to the project team. They are also required to complete additional project-related tasks, such as reviewing data and attending training. List what you need colleagues to do to make the change successful. These requirements can become burdensome because different project teams rarely coordinate their schedules so that activities don't overlap, requiring colleagues to manage many tasks at the same time. Multiple requests can lead to productivity declines that will affect their ability to achieve deliverables.

The level of executive commitment and support is also of critical importance. There are three indicators to watch out for. First, have leaders demonstrated a keen interest in the change? Second, do they have the capacity to visibly lead their teams through the transition? If they don't, then regardless of how much they like the project, they won't be around when you need them. Third, are the deliverables aligned with the organization's strategy? If they aren't, leaders probably will not be able to sustain the required support over the project's duration.

Finally, you need to know your staff. Are they highly capable teams that have successfully managed changes like this in the past? Conversely, are they new teams that lack the capabilities to take on the change?

By assessing these factors you'll have a good idea of what you are getting into and what realistic project deliverables you can sign up for.

Thumbs Down, Thumbs Up

In 2009, Cadbury adopted a more centralized structure by removing its regional operations and having the country divisions report directly to the global organization. This transition was part of a company-wide cost-reduction program to help achieve mid-teen-percent profit margins by 2011.

After the change was implemented, however, a review revealed that staff costs had actually gone up—more people were hired and more promotions had been granted. What the initial change project had assumed was that the central group had the power to enforce cost savings, which wasn't necessarily the case. Because of existing governance, the project was at risk of not achieving its goals even before it started. In hindsight, it was clear that the savings could have been delivered only by the leaders who had control over budgets, which were still decentralized.

👍 In 2004, Boeing, the giant American aerospace and defense company, formed a project team at its C-17 production facility in Long Beach, California, to address employee safety concerns and high workers' compensation costs. In the Figuring It Out phase, the team reviewed injury data (e.g., why workers' compensation costs increased 74 percent from 2002 to 2003), benchmarked performance at Boeing's C-17 facility versus other Boeing sites and aerospace companies, and conducted an employee safety survey to determine the gap between current and best-in-class performance. Also, stakeholder needs were quantified based on the ability to influence the project. The team used a change readiness tool to assess the likelihood of project success, given the objectives set (injury reduction and safety improvement by 25 percent in year one). These objectives were supported by an external consultant with experience in safety management systems. One year after the program was put in place, the recordable injury rate was down 32 percent, the lost workday rate reduced by 46 percent, and the safety survey scores up by 25 percent.

What Works

- Ask your stakeholders, your team, and yourself, "What has to be true to be successful?" Then gauge how aligned these requirements are with the environment in which you're working.

- Compare your initiative with similar projects to ensure the deliverables are realistic.

- Confirm the amount of decision-making power you will have in the project. Your degree of autonomy will impact the outcomes you can realistically sign up for.

- Discuss challenges and roadblocks with the executive sponsor before you commit to deliverables.

- Discuss the level of readiness of the organization to take on the project. Will your project be supported if times get tough? Is this a must-do initiative or a nice-to-do side project?

Deliverables and the resources you have to achieve them are two sides of the same equation. If they match, you can feel confident about what you have been asked to do. If the resources don't match the deliverables, you need to share your research with the executive sponsor to either get more resources or modify the deliverables. When deliverables and resources are balanced you can start thinking about the measures that will demonstrate your progress toward achieving the project's goals.

CHAPTER 8

How Do I Measure Success?

Companies can't accelerate what they don't measure.
—DeAnne Aguirre

DEFINING HOW SUCCESS WILL BE MEASURED is critical at the start of your project. These metrics will measure how your change project is performing, along with you as a leader.

Leaders will have their own views about appropriate measures of success. Like other aspects of the project plan, it is best to provide them with a recommendation of what you think is best for the project. By doing so you narrow the conversation to the few you believe are the best choices for your deliverables. The more tied to business goals, the more weight they will have with leaders and the easier they will be to track. Be careful about metrics that can be affected by factors beyond the project's control. Include these without caveats and you will be constantly recalibrating results, and this will dampen positive results and intensify negative ones.

Thumbs Down, Thumbs Up

👎 In 2000, when Cadbury Chocolate Canada acquired Trebor Allan, the newly merged company became the largest confectionery company in Canada. The project team had combined the two businesses as planned, but, after 14 months, it was missing its goals. A new leader asked the team if the merger was successful, and the members said, "yes." He then asked, "How do you know?" Since the team had not identified specific measures of success for the merger other than annual financial targets, members could only claim that the plan was executed (citing anecdotal evidence), which didn't answer the question. The silence in the room was palpable.

👍 Telefónica de Argentina is that country's largest fixed-line telephone provider. The company had outsourced its accounts payable for its 800 advertising suppliers to a media agency. In 2008, only 2 percent of invoices were being paid on time, resulting in angry suppliers, difficult rate negotiations, and negative comments in the press. Telefónica embarked on a quality-improvement project to identify and eliminate problems within its payment process. It was called "Mission Possible."

The project manager aligned her objectives with three strategic plan objectives: improving efficiency to help generate growth and increase profits, maintaining "best place to work" status, and improving public positioning. Stakeholders included all internal and external parties— internal consisted of quality, marketing, management control, accounts payable, communications, the CEO, and executive team; external consisted of its media agency, 800 media suppliers, and nonmedia suppliers. All stakeholders were communicated with regularly and were given progress updates against plan milestones.

Many causes of delays were identified, including lack of preapproved budgets, unnecessary payment authorizations, no submission deadlines, and duplicate invoices. Key stakeholders were invited to brainstorm potential solutions and evaluate options. The project team received approval for its recommendation by demonstrating to the executive team how it met objectives in Telefónica's strategic plan (including over $3 million in savings). Stakeholders were invited to help define changes to existing procedures, and the new process was tested during a two-month pilot project to correct inefficiencies. The project team achieved its objectives, including increasing on-time payments from 2 to 97.5 percent, recovery of $1.7 million in tax credits, an increase in employee satisfaction from 36 to more than 85 percent, and an increase in supplier satisfaction from 28 to 86 percent.

What Works

- Include hard (data) and soft (anecdotal) measurements. The hard ones suggest organizational progress; the soft, personal benefits and evidence of alignment.

- Select metrics that confirm colleagues are able to use new processes or systems versus ones that just measure them being installed. Some consultants encourage measuring "the solution being provided," which is like a furnace technician being measured on a furnace being installed and in working order without the owners knowing how it works or having instructions to read (and therefore running the risk of freezing to death).

- Decide what you want your success to be compared against—external benchmarks, industry specific targets, internal goals, and so on.

- Ensure you measure the current state of the organization so you can demonstrate improvement.

- Make sure the data is easily obtainable. Spending significant resources compiling data that isn't near at hand is a waste of time and energy.

- Gain input from the project team on your recommended approach to measuring success before presenting it to the executive sponsor and the rest of the leadership team. Their operational perspectives may uncover a better option.

- Get sign-offs on the measurements and key performance indicators before you begin implementing the project.

- Track metrics weekly on a well-publicized summary chart, often referred to as a dashboard. This allows you to take corrective action quickly and identify accomplishments. You can track progress by milestones reached and the time it took to reach them.

Defining clear and obtainable metrics will confirm your achievements, simplify reporting, and provide you with data to verify when the project is on track or when remedial actions are necessary. Sharing this data with key stakeholders will increase their engagement and encourage their participation when needed. Once you have all the information required to get your head around the project, you need to review everything you have discovered to make sure that the change will achieve the desired outcomes.

Metrics List

Desired Outcome	Measurement	Current Baseline	Goal	Frequency of Measurement
Increased customer service	Number of customer problems resolved in the first customer call with technician	20%	50%	Weekly
Reduced call time	Length of customer call	7 minutes	5 minutes	Weekly
Increased customer survey responses	Number of customers who complete an online survey	35%	60%	Weekly

*http://www.changewithconfidence.com/?page_id=95

CHAPTER 9

Will the Change Actually Achieve the Desired Outcome?

The great enemy of the truth is very often not the lie, deliberate, contrived and dishonest, but the myth, persistent, persuasive and unrealistic.

—**John F. Kennedy**

A program that has not been thoroughly vetted is doomed to mediocrity, if not failure.

—**Abdullatif A. Al-Othman**

EACH COMPANY HAS CULTURAL MYTHS built upon past lore, present optimism, and future dreams. At the beginning of a big change project, speed becomes the new currency, and to avoid looking like they can't keep up, most people put their heads down and just keep working. As a change leader, before you dive into early planning activities, step back to see if your project will deliver the desired outcomes. If the answer is "no," you will not succeed. Unless, of course, you change the parameters; that is, shift the goal posts or change the game.

Often projects are decided upon without a thorough analysis of the facts or a consideration of alternative—often less dramatic—solutions.

Thinking through these high-level questions will better prepare you for conversations with key stakeholders and lead to follow-on strategic questions, such as, "What is the real issue we are trying to solve?", "How do we know?", "What are the options to solve it?", and "What is the best option to do so?" Addressing these questions up front will ensure you are on the right track or signal a need for realignment. Testing organizational myths will save you from the bigger challenge of not living up to them at the end of the project.

Thumbs Down, Thumbs Up

At the height of his popularity in the 1970s, Greg Lake, a member of the English progressive rock group Emerson, Lake, & Palmer, commissioned a special guitar to be built, a guitar that could do anything he wanted to on stage. He commissioned a custom two-neck model that included the latest in amplifiers, whammy bars, and tuning options. He visited the manufacturer when it was ready and found that all his specifications had been incorporated. The only problem was that the guitar was too heavy to hold long enough to play a song.

Cadbury had progressively increased its investment in new product development for years as a way of increasing sales. A project team was formed to find ways of increasing innovation effectiveness, and its review of active projects revealed that there were hundreds of new product initiatives being worked on. But most of them were low in value, a trend that had been growing for years. Even worse, new products were being worked on by multiple teams in different locations. This data triggered the development of a more centralized approach to innovation that focused on "fewer, faster, bigger, better" projects. It wasn't easy to move innovation accountability from local to global teams, but after a couple of years the change resulted in significant sales increases. A new and more effective approach was created by challenging conventional wisdom. Creating more innovation projects was not the best answer to achieve the desired outcome of more sales.

What Works

- Do your own research and talk to as many people as possible. These interactions will give you a clear understanding of the situation and enable you to start building relationships with stakeholders.

- Consider the degree of alignment between the project and the organization's mission, values, and long-term strategy.

- Determine if there is a history of finishing big change projects and achieving the objectives that were initially set.

- Ask about how the consumer, customer, and supplier will be affected by the change. Are there any potential issues associated with the change that will impede the project's success?

- Ask yourself, "If I were an investor, would I support this project given the costs and promised returns?"

For your project to be successful, the changes you make need to deliver the prescribed outcomes. I have seen projects that executed the changes well but failed because they didn't produce the desired benefits. "Make sure the tool (the change) is right for the job (your outcomes)" is a wise adage to live by before you begin planning. You must test the beliefs and assumptions around the project with your own facts and data.

CHAPTER 10

How Do I Avoid Scope Creep?

There is no such thing as scope creep, only scope gallop.
—**Cornelius Fichtner**

The conditions attached to a promise are forgotten; only the promise is remembered.
—**Harold Kerzner**

OFTEN THE ORIGINAL SCOPE of a project expands without any consideration for necessary additional resources or required timeline changes. Scope creep can involve increasing breadth (such as increasing the number of software modules) or depth (expanding the audience to include more teams). It is easy for a leadership team to increase specifications of software programs or extend the reach of efficiency drives without considering what additional investment is required to deliver the new benefits. They can quickly assume that the bigger the scope, the bigger the benefits, with no additional resources required—which is rarely the case. Once you agree to a scope increase, the old one is forgotten, and you are suddenly in new perceptual terrain: if you miss milestones, the increased scope will not be seen as a good reason for not achieving your project's objectives.

Thumbs Down, Thumbs Up

👎 In 2001, McDonald's began designing a digital network–based operating system called "Innovate" for its finance, human resources, and supply chain applications. The new system would replace all of its major back-office systems and provide real-time information on its 30,000 restaurants through an intranet browser. Sales, staffing, and inventory data would be available 24/7. The project scope expanded to include kitchen equipment operations that would report on things such as the temperature of each fryer and carbon dioxide levels in soda machines. Designers also envisioned connectivity with McDonald's 300-plus approved vendors. (For example, historical data could be provided to a freezer technician to help him or her diagnose a malfunction.) They also built in connectivity for employee training and productivity tools, which were originally outside the plan.

The five-year, $1-billion project was terminated in less than two years, having lost $1.7 million. The scope was so broad that there was no way of building the system. As well, the decision to transition all 30,000 restaurants to the new system at one time added to the project's complexity, even though break-even benefits would have been realized when its eight top-performing stores were operational. Shortly afterward, the CEO told shareholders that its focus was now on improving the quality of its products.

👍 The Cadbury Adams USA and Canada commercial teams were moving to a common IT platform in 2005 to complete the Adams merger. In the planning stage, the project team suggested that the manufacturing plants move to the new system, too. They reasoned that more benefits would be realized if more business areas were put onto the one system. The manufacturing leader countered with a case for not participating in the project because he was in the middle of launching an efficiency initiative. Also, the project team did not have the capability or the bandwidth to take on this additional work. Manufacturing delayed its transition to the new system for three years, once their other change project was completed. A significant risk to the business was avoided by not increasing the scope of a project beyond that which the project team could manage.

What Works

- Create a one-page project charter (see chart on the next page) that details background and context, outcomes and deliverables, resources, objectives, metrics, stakeholders, scope, and milestones (what and when). Asking the project team members to edit it is a great way of engaging them and setting up a participatory culture. People support what they create, and the editing process will generate buy-in. It is best to review the plan with your executive sponsor and allow for input before it is shared with the leadership team.

- Review the charter with the leadership team, even if they say it's not necessary. You may have to refer back to this meeting to defend against scope changes or to lobby for additional resources.

- Share your project's scope with the business teams that are undergoing the change. The more that is generally known, the harder it is to increase the project scope without additional resources.

- Gain agreement that all charter changes (including scope) will be reviewed by the leadership team. Potential additional resource requirements must be part of the discussion.

- Clearly define the process for reviewing change requests. A thorough review process will discourage ad hoc requests. If this approach is new to your organization, offer your project as a test, especially if people have voiced concerns about too many projects being run simultaneously.

- Document all scope changes. You may need to make a case that many small changes are resulting in significant resource issues.

- Raise requests to increase project requirements right away. Inactivity may imply that they are not an issue, and it's almost impossible to refute "Why didn't you raise this earlier if it's such a significant issue?"

- Embrace scope changes with the approval of additional resources: you need to demonstrate reasonable flexibility. If you get a mandated scope change without additional resources, try to change the timeline of the project.

Project Charter

Background/Context (Business Need)	Outcomes and Deliverables	Resources (People and Budget)
– Ten years ago, the company defined its mission and corporate values – In March 2010, an employee survey revealed that colleagues believe that the mission and values need to be modernized to reflect current realities	– A recommendation on whether or not to modernize the company mission and values – A strategy for embedding the new mission and values	– Project manager – Corporate affairs representative – One external consultant experienced in corporate culture development – Work team of "top talent" leaders from different departments and geographies

Objectives	Key Performance Indicators	Stakeholders
– Assess the merits of modernizing the company's mission and values – Develop an approach to embed the company's mission and values into fabric of colleagues' ways of working	– Colleague survey scores – Focus group feedback – Employment offers accepted (percent)	– Executive sponsor – Leadership team members – Corporate Affairs

Scope		Milestones (What and When)	
IN	**OUT**		
– Mission and values – All geographies and business groups	– Company purpose – Joint venture groups	– Sign off project charter with leadership team	December 15
		– Hold focus groups	January–February
		– Conduct external benchmarking	January 31
		– Review research with leadership team	March 1
		– Develop recommendation	March–April
		– Review recommendation	April 24

*http://www.changewithconfidence.com/?page_id=102

(This can be dangerous because if agreed to, you'll need to reset your project plan—additional work that could suggest the project is not going well.)

- Offer to defer the scope change to phase two of the project, even if one doesn't currently exist.

Properly resourced scope changes can add substantial value to the business. They can also destroy value if not resourced properly. A thorough review process is your best defense against unprofitable additions.

The "Figuring It Out" phase of a change project gives you an overall understanding of the size and complexity of the task. It enables you to assess what must change in your organization for your project to be successful and what resources you will need. Also, it ensures that the initiative makes sense and is aligned with overall business strategies. When you have sufficiently explored the parameters of your project you can focus your efforts on planning for the change based on the achievable scope and deliverables you have agreed to.

PART 2

Planning for Change

ONCE YOU HAVE FINISHED "FIGURING IT OUT," you have to develop a sense of the nature of the change and a set of expectations for deliverables, and create a plan that defines how you will transition colleagues and the business through to your desired post-change state. This involves breaking down the change into sequenced activities and defining the resources required to implement them, and selling the plan to your stakeholders and communicating it to your organization.

The Plan

CHAPTER 11

What Does a Good Plan Look Like?

A good plan is like a road map: it shows the final destination and the best way to get there.

—H. Stanley Judd

IT IS FAR EASIER TO IMPLEMENT a change once you have a strong plan to guide your actions—a detailed plan that maps out the project activities and provides a framework for leaders and the project team to follow. The plan is also a major communications vehicle and a central repository for all modifications that occur during implementation. It should operationalize the project charter and include details on deliverables, budget, resources, and timelines.

Often at the beginning of a big change project, "speed" becomes the mantra and you feel like you have fallen behind even before you have started. It takes courage to resist the pressure to execute before dedicating the necessary time to creating a solid plan of how you will achieve your deliverables. Once the plan is agreed to, then, and only then, can you and your team implement it with speed.

Thumbs Down, Thumbs Up

In 2007, Cadbury Schweppes split itself in two businesses, spinning off its beverages division from the confectionery group. It was an intense time for the company because Nelson Peltz, an activist shareholder, had purchased a sizable amount of the corporation's stock and was making demands of the management.

A core element of the demerger was the division of the global IT group into separate global confectionery and Americas Beverages teams. The newly appointed external project manager pressured his team to create a change plan within a week, even though the scope of the project had not yet been approved. The plan was submitted on time, but it was filled with cut-and-paste content from past project plans and generic descriptions of change models. The plan was approved but not understood or used. The team's time would have been much better spent building a genuine plan rather than submitting a useless shell.

When Cadbury Adams USA harmonized its computer systems in 2004, the sponsor of the project insisted that each work team be assigned a responsibility for the project to have a plan, even when the information required to build it was not yet available. He believed that they needed to create the skeleton of a plan, filling in the blanks once information became available. His motto was "Get a plan, argue a plan, get a better plan."

When the first drafts of the change plans were presented to him, he poked holes in them and looked for small cracks where weaknesses hadn't been considered. This was something the team didn't expect—after all, it was only a draft—but the feedback helped the team identify areas in need of additional attention and prioritized outstanding decisions to be made, which led to a better plan. Creating the work-in-progress drafts helped identify gaps and encouraged the continuous improvement of the plan.

What Works

Process

- Create a project summary to test your understanding of details and guide the project's shape before others try to do so. You don't want stakeholders planning for you or to be spending time assessing other people's ideas.

- Publish numbered versions of your plan so the team knows which is current and when changes have been made.

- Allow for flexibility in implementation, and leave the minute details to the teams that have to make the change.

- Calibrate your plan with the resources available to deliver it. Don't take on what you can't deliver with your project team.

Content and Structure

- Keep your plan simple and focused. The longer your plan is, the less likely it will be absorbed (or even read) by colleagues who need to follow it.

- Break the project down into distinct phases with specific goals. This allows for better communication, helps focus colleagues on short-term objectives, and enables you to show momentum (e.g., "Phase two is complete and we are moving into phase three").

- Ensure that phase one is planned in detail.

- State your assumptions in every part of your plan (scope, resources, timeline, etc.). This will allow you to make changes if your assumptions are incorrect.

- When teams request making changes to software or processes to meet their specific needs, support only those that will make a marked productivity improvement.

- Include interdependencies between different parts of the plan. Delays in one activity will cause delays in others.

- Insist that every activity has someone responsible for it.

- Build in project checkpoints at key milestones to stay on track. If you are not on track, determine the activities that will get you on schedule and build them into the plan.

- To save time and avoid confusion, use templates that have worked on other projects.

Stakeholder Alignment

- Make sure stakeholders agree with your definition of what a good change plan looks like and the information required to complete it.

- Describe your change plan as a work in progress that will be modified as decisions are made and information becomes available. The project needs to be dynamic and flexible to deliver maximum results.

- Test the plan with leaders to make sure the assumptions behind it are reasonable and to see what is missing.

- Build in a leadership team project review meeting after each major milestone. This will allow you to inform the team of changes to the plan, remind it of what is coming up, and receive feedback.

- Distribute a written plan to ensure that all stakeholders and project team members are operating under the same assumptions and using the same information. The following topic areas will provide a solid basis for your plan.

Project Plan

Table of Contents
Context/background
Objectives
Scope (in/out)
Outcomes/deliverables (including measurements)
Approach (required changes to behaviors, process, capabilities, and technology)
Assumptions
Risks/interdependencies
Governance
Timeline
Resources
Budget

*http://www.changewithconfidence.com/?page_id=107

Your project plan is the most important document of your change project. It lays out the path you will follow to achieve success. It is also a tool for aligning people based on what resources you need. Successful projects always have good change plans.

CHAPTER 12

How Do I Get the Budget to Do It Right?

Allocating ample resources is a telltale sign to the organization that the effort is a true priority.

—**Linda Ackerman Anderson and Dean Anderson**

WITHOUT ADEQUATE RESOURCES to support your change, you will be faced with trade-offs that often lead to a poor transition to new ways of working and a burned-out team. There is a natural tension between resource needs and their availability, and your initial bottom-up tally of requirements may well be challenged. This tension often becomes more intense as the project progresses because there are usually cost overruns due to unexpected needs or delays. Technical resources tend to be easier to justify than those supporting people transition because they are more tangible. Leaders typically understand that computer programming is required to install a new system, but some may feel that leadership coaching is not essential or even necessary. This is a mistake.

Spending time creating a fact-based resourcing plan will enable you to confidently have funding discussions before the change is implemented and make adjustments to the project plan to manage shortfalls.

Thumbs Down, Thumbs Up

In 2004 the village of Oak Park, west of Chicago, Illinois—former home of novelist Ernest Hemingway and architect Frank Lloyd Wright—bought a computer system for $1.65 million to manage its payroll and finances. The system appeared to be too complex for this small organization and the aggressive implementation schedule hadn't budgeted for basic computer skills training. Also, the leadership team had not budgeted for the staff or maintenance costs to run the system. The village operations manager concluded, "We would normally need at least two full-time people, one in IT, and one in Finance, to focus exclusively on this software, in addition to the ongoing fees, product updates, and tools needed to keep it going."[1] After five years and a $2-million investment, the village abandoned the software package. A disaster!

In 2005, Cadbury Schweppes launched a global program designed to transform how the company made strategic commercial decisions. In terms of ambition and scope it was the biggest skills-building initiative in the history of the company: "To have the most sought after growth capability program in the blue chip, packaged goods industry within five years"[2] was the goal.

The Canadian project team proposed that the project be launched as a company-wide business transformation instead of just a commercial training program. The leadership team agreed and approved a larger budget that included money for leadership facilitation and coaching, a broader audience for training, and strong communications support. Over the next two years it completely reshaped the language and culture of the organization. There was excitement around the events and a feeling that the company was championing a new era. The project team received extra funding because it successfully identified the opportunity to transform core ways of working to drive better results, and it negotiated the resourcing budget to do so effectively.

What Works

- Build in a reserve allowance of 5 to 10 percent for unknown expenses or inaccurate cost assumptions. This will avoid renegotiating and losing face because you didn't predict the need.

- Build in a small provision for ongoing support after the change has been implemented to ensure that the new ways of working stick. Ensure you have a distinct budget for your project versus the department owning it. (Otherwise you'll spend a lot of time developing updates and justifying reallocations of funds to areas that need them most.)

- Review lessons learned from change initiatives launched over the past few years.

- Assess whether your project overlaps with the deliverables of an existing project. If so, make a case for shared resources.

- If some elements of your budget are not approved, be clear about the activities you will not be able to fund. There is a possibility that they will be approved during the project when these activities are needed.

One of the biggest challenges during the "Planning for Change" phase is building and negotiating the project budget. If your project is underfunded, important activities will not be done, and you likely will not be able to make the changes required for success. Rigorous analysis will help you develop and negotiate the budget needed to achieve your deliverables. Once you have secured your project resources you can start planning how the project will be run.

CHAPTER 13

What Governance Is Required to Run the Project?

Rules are not necessarily sacred; principles are.
—Franklin D. Roosevelt

"Governance" in this context means the managerial rules that guide how work is done. Structure and order are necessary at the start of a big change project: people need to understand how their roles contribute to the project and what is expected of them. Creating these rules confidently and quickly will signal that you are in charge and have the capabilities to run the project, and you'll be able to embed behaviors required for the change to happen within your governance structure.

Establishing how the project will be governed is the first discussion you must have with the leadership team or project steering committee (that may include additional people who can guide and support the project). Leaders and project team members need to know their roles and responsibilities, what meetings they must attend, how decisions will be made, and how issues and risks will be managed. If you don't define the rules within a week or so of the project kickoff, people will fill in the vacuum according to their past experiences or preferences. It is a lot harder to move people away from their communicated positions on governance than it is to get them aligned with your governance proposal. You need to quickly develop it, review it, and then cement it into the project.

Roles and responsibilities must be clear and should not overlap. What is each person accountable for (e.g., attending weekly project meetings, providing progress updates, deadlines for feedback, and so on)? What is their contribution? What are their deliverables? You need to document these details in writing and review them with everyone involved in the project. This will avoid anyone saying "I wasn't aware of this" or "The IT department didn't sign up for that," and so on.

Decision-making criteria are critical to good governance. There is a tendency to be unspecific about who makes decisions and how they will be made, and vagueness will lead to project delays, anger, and, sometimes, resentment. Discussing these rules up front will provide room for debate before decisions must be made, and establishing protocols for each type of decision (e.g., approval to proceed to the next phase of the project, requests for more resources, etc.) will make it clear how decisions are made. For example, a protocol on who attends training could be: "All colleagues who operate the new software will receive training on their procedures." This may seem like simple common sense, but if these principles are not agreed to at the beginning of the project, there will be confusion and friction when decisions need to be made.

Fight hard to enforce principles, and be flexible about everything else. Leaders naturally wish to customize activities to meet their needs. As long as they stay within the principles, you'll have the consistency you need and can provide the flexibility they need. Let them customize elements that will not threaten the success of the project. They are the best qualified to do so.

Thumbs Down, Thumbs Up

AR Accessories Group is a leading leather goods manufacturer known for inventing industry-standard features like the spare key pocket and card and photo holders for wallets. In 1996, the U.S. company decided to upgrade its computer system and reengineer its business processes to help fight international competition from low-cost manufacturers in Asia entering its home market.

The project began with little vision of where the company was going, and there were few goals with which to align the project. Also, no project timeline was agreed to, other than a directional launch date of "after the busy retail season." Since there were no milestones and tracking procedures, the team worked long hours without any formal approach for resolving issues, or for presenting them to the leadership team. Two critical milestones were completely missed—the confirmation of the project's scope and the finalizing of the system design—and without these in place, new processes and programming requirements were constantly being added to the project. The initiative ran over budget and did not achieve its original business case for purchasing the new computer system.

When Cadbury Schweppes merged with Adams in 2003, the process for assigning new roles was governed by a set of principles created by the Human Resources department and approved by the leadership team. For example, if two candidates appeared equally qualified for a role, an external agency would conduct assessments of both and present these to the hiring committee. These guidelines were communicated to all colleagues, and concerns about specific appointments were addressed by demonstrating how the process had been followed. People may not have had their favorite candidates placed in key roles, but they could not fault the appointments process, and the new leadership team gained trust because of this transparency.

What Works

Principles and Protocols

- Demonstrate governance in a visual format, as doing so shows how things are connected and is easy to understand. (See the following chart for examples.)
- Include business and people-related principles:
  - Maintain business performance throughout the change project. It provides a common-sense check when leaders or the project team consider options that are not in the best interests of the organization.
  - Treat people with respect, dignity, and fairness. Setting a high bar for conduct is the right thing to do, and it enables leaders to justify their decisions.

Organization Design Process

	Shared Services Talent Review	Organization Structure	Assignment of Talent	Structure Alignment
	May 21–22	May 22–28	May 30–31	June 6–7
Objective	Understand talent profiles of all colleagues (no structure)	Draft organization structures (no names)	Assign talent to boxes	Final review of org Design and talent assignment
Deliverable	Finalize colleague factbook	Draft final organization design (no names)	Final organization design with draft names	Final organization design with final names
Owners	Sponsor (Functional head)	Department heads	Department heads	Functional head Department heads Human Resources head
Support	Change managers Human Resources Business partner	Change managers	Change managers	Change managers
Agenda	– Complete and validate data – Define criteria for skill assessment – Map colleagues according to HR principles	– Map out roles by area	– Assign talent to roles according to HR principles and role requirements	– Assign talent between two new companies – Confirm other assignments
Location	Head Office	Virtual	Virtual	Head Office

*http://www.changewithconfidence.com/?page_id=113

- Communicate how teams have customized implementation activities to meet their needs (as long as they are consistent with the project's guiding principles). This will reward colleagues for their participation in driving the change and encourage other teams to do the same, while also improving the overall perception of the project.

Decision Rights

- Recommend principles to be used as decision-making criteria throughout the project. Ideally, the leadership team will tweak them before they are approved, which will increase that team's combined ownership of the decision-making process.

- To ensure leaders are clear on decision rights, present real-life scenarios to demonstrate how decisions will be made and what the consequences of potential decisions will be. Outline who has input and who makes the final call. If you miss this step, some people will naturally interpret decision-making rules in their favor, which will cause disputes and distract stakeholders.

Meetings

- Set ground rules for project meetings so they are efficient and effective. These rules commonly encompass attendance at meetings, turnaround time for feedback, and agenda and presentation formats.

- Send out meeting invites as soon as the dates are set. This will communicate a sense of urgency to stakeholders and project team members.

- Insist that stakeholders send substitutes if they are unable to attend a meeting, and that substitutes be active participants acting on their behalf.

- Circulate notes from all meetings within 24 hours. People will interpret details of agreements differently if you don't have a mechanism to ensure accuracy. A protocol stating that notes must be reviewed and any corrections forwarded within 48 hours is also useful.

- Build a meeting schedule. This is an excellent way to spark governance discussions, identify gaps, and gain approvals. Feedback should be encouraged so that any gaps can be filled in prior to seeking sign-off.

Meeting Schedule

Meeting	Attendees	Focus	Outputs
Steering Committee Meeting third Monday of every month	• Leadership team • Team members as required	• Progress on upcoming milestone • Issues that need executive involvement and approvals	• List of risks • List of issues • List of decisions made

*http://www.changewithconfidence.com/?page_id=115

Processes

- Make it clear that processes are owned by the business. Encouraging business ownership ensures that the best people are making decisions—the ones with the most knowledge and interest in making the change work.

Data

- Gain agreement on what data will be tracked and by whom.
- Create concise update protocols. Over time, many leadership team members will resort to skimming the content or, even worse, not reviewing it at all. If you're using a consulting company's documentation procedures, make sure they make sense for your project.

Governance principles and protocols are the rules of the road for your change project. Your role, like a police officer's, is to ensure people follow them so the organization's best interests are upheld. You need to intervene quickly if you see people (especially leaders) breaking agreed-upon rules, so that order can be reestablished.

Once you have your governance model developed and approved, you can dive into the meat of the "Planning for Change" phase: defining how you will build the capabilities of colleagues to enable the change to occur.

CHAPTER 14

How Do I Prepare People to Work in New Ways?

When resistance, in the form of fear, anger, or complacency,
is in the way, true learning cannot occur.
—Dan S. Cohen

MOST BIG CHANGES require new ways of working: a combination of new knowledge, skills, mind-sets, behaviors, relationships, and processes must be adopted. Unless you accurately identify and build these capabilities, the change is certain to fail or not reach its potential.

Once you identify what needs to change, determine how best to prepare colleagues to adopt it. You will need to build a plan for introducing new ways of working for all impacted colleagues. Change happens when people discuss and practise the new ways of working, and your plan should center on these activities. Furthermore, change has not fully happened until colleagues habitually use new ways of working (and forget they are new). The better job you do building capabilities, the better prepared colleagues will be and the greater the confidence they will have to follow them.

Thumbs Down, Thumbs Up

London Heathrow Terminal 5 opened with great fanfare in 2008. Queen Elizabeth II spoke at a special ceremony two weeks before it opened to the public. She enthused about the "bright, airy space and clean, efficient layout" and referred to it as the "twenty-first century gateway to

Britain and, for us, the wider world."[1] Its main building was the largest free-standing structure in the United Kingdom and had the capacity to handle 35 million passengers annually. It was run by a complex set of 163 different computer systems with 546 interfaces between them.

On opening day, Europe's largest baggage system failed and British Airways was forced to cancel 34 flights. Over the next 10 days, 500 flights were canceled and 42,000 bags were misdirected. Analysis of this start-up failure pointed to a lack of capability as the main reason for the disaster. "Getting people to understand the new role of technology and buy-in to the new proposition was our biggest challenge,"[2] said British Airway's IT program head for Terminal 5. Although training was conducted over the year prior to opening, it wasn't sufficient to operate the new systems or to properly educate staff on the new ways of working.

👍 Texas Children's Hospital is one of 76 facilities ranked in at least one specialty in the annual *U.S. News* Children's Best Hospital report. The teaching hospital embarked on a four-year change project to move from paper-based to electronic medical records. The end goal was to provide easy access to patient records and information from any department of the hospital. Two departments transitioned first, with one making a significantly greater investment in building capabilities than the other. The first group held project roadshows attended by leaders. Ongoing update forums were held through live web meetings to share the latest updates, profile the functionality of the system, and discuss issues, and an employee computer portal was set up to give easy access to all documentation. Also, when colleagues transitioned to the new system, they used a dedicated support team for ongoing training. Both groups transitioned, but the first group (with superior capabilities support) scored far higher in its preparedness for moving to the new electronic system.

What Works

Design

Nominate someone responsible for each process being changed. This person must help design and deliver the training and ensure nothing falls through the cracks.

Document capability requirements and the support needed to develop them. Sometimes people will be offered to the project, but they might lack the knowledge or skills to lead the training. It is best to negotiate hard for the right resources, and this document will help you make the case.

Capability Plan

Group	Number to Be Trained	Capability Requirement	Support Required (training, coaching, etc.)	When	Led By
Science and Technology	3	New product feasibility	One-day process course	April 5	• One manager knowledgeable about the innovation process and tracking software • One technical trainer
Marketing	5				
Innovation	2				
Total	10				
Marketing	15	Collaborative planning	One- to two-hour webcast	May 10	• One external facilitator
Sales	40				
Total	55				

*http://www.changewithconfidence.com/?page_id=119

- Training works best when it progresses from creating awareness to building skills to enabling practices. Start with awareness sessions to communicate what is changing and what will be different in the post-change world. Move next to capability development, which should encompass the knowledge, skills, and behaviors required to make the change successful. Finally, there should be reinforcement in the form of team practice sessions to build familiarity and comfort with the new ways of working.

- Provide step-by-step job aids for critical processes, such as how to allocate stock to customers, especially those that involve people in different locations or from different teams.

Training Pyramid

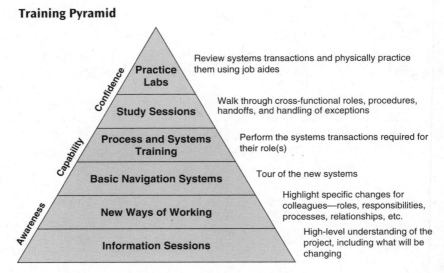

*http://www.changewithconfidence.com/?page_id=121

- Before the launch provide an overview of how colleagues will be supported (on-site technical support, job aids, help lines, etc.) and when handoffs between people doing process steps will be made.

- Make training fun. Studies have shown that people learn and retain more when they are enjoying themselves.

- Create a single site to house all documents related to the project.

Delivery

- Schedule briefing sessions with managers before training begins. This will help them answer questions their team members may have and reinforce the importance of attending sessions.

- Ensure everyone impacted by the change receives training, and encourage leaders to attend training sessions to demonstrate that attendance is a priority.

- Secure internal process experts to lead training sessions. This will make your training more relevant and allow questions to be answered based on how the organization operates.

- Ensure external trainers, if used, are briefed on how the organization operates (including relationships and interdependencies). Without this context the training will be compromised.

- Allow enough time in your agenda for colleague feedback on the new processes. They may detect process gaps missed by the design team.

Training Scheduling

- Make training mandatory. If not, some people will avoid attending sessions to focus on other priorities.

- Secure enough space to hold scheduled training and a few extra catch-up sessions.

- Ideally, hold training sessions close to when colleagues will need to use what they have learned. However, sometimes training sessions need to be held months before the change is made (often because of the large number of colleagues needing to be trained). If this is the case, hold quick refresher sessions just before the launch.

- Ensure managers and their teams are scheduled for the same training sessions. They will learn more, especially vis-à-vis applications within their own environment.

- Track attendance to training and vigilantly follow up with those who miss sessions, so that they get rescheduled.

- Send out invites as soon as the schedule is set. This provides a sense of magnitude and momentum for your project.

- Ensure that the schedule is not so condensed that participants can't manage their roles. If it is, you'll have many no-shows.

The heart of your capability plan is defining what needs to change for colleagues to work in the post-change environment and how you will prepare them to do so. Once you build a detailed plan, you need to anticipate risks that could endanger it.

CHAPTER 15

How Do I Reduce Risk?

*Top executives consistently overestimate benefits
and underestimate risks.*

—**Margaret Wente**

THERE ARE SUBSTANTIAL RISKS associated with every big business change. Your project plan is probably largely based on past experiences and the information you have to date, but new circumstances or unanticipated events (or negative reactions) can wreak havoc with it. You need to pressure-test your plan *and* plan for things that can go wrong. It's like *Mission: Impossible,* or at least you'll often feel that way: "Your job, should you choose to accept it," is to identify risks, mitigate them before the launch, and build in contingency plans (in case the risks materialize).

There are two types of risk: technical risks (for example, when an IT system is not operating the way it should) and people risks (for example, sales representatives not being knowledgeable about a new ordering process). From my experience, technical risks get a lot of attention and are well documented and people risks much less so. This is a mistake.

Thumbs Down, Thumbs Up

When Cadbury Adams USA upgraded its computer systems, the project team requested that each department develop risk and contingency plans. However, when a major issue occurred in the third-party distribution warehouses, the contingency plan was not sufficiently detailed to manage the situation. Some of the configuration requirements were incorrect, and the supplier's employees had not been adequately trained. A "SWAT" team was flown to the warehouses, which, to their credit, had been doing their best to ship products. The challenges were resolved after a few months, but significant additional financial costs had been incurred and the company's reputation took a hit.

Contingency plans were developed during the planning stage of the Kraft Foods merger with Cadbury. Initially, the focus was on technical risks, such as an inability to generate invoices, but shortly thereafter, people risks were reviewed and five key areas were assessed: leadership, culture, resistance, capability, and teamwork. The two global change leaders held workshops with 20 national leadership teams to identify and mitigate people risks to their business. National divisions in countries as diverse as Russia and Brazil had similar people risks, confirming the hypothesis that change management issues are universal. Conducting senior, cross-departmental risk sessions ensured that risks were acknowledged and plans were supported.

What Works

Content

- Create contingency plans for risks to the overall business and for each group impacted.
- Ask each department to brainstorm possible risks and then validate the list with a cross-departmental team.
- Identify risks caused by project plan interdependencies. Develop plans for all potential delays (of machine delivery, inability to complete training on time, etc.).
- Ensure that all external stakeholders (customers, consumers, suppliers, government, and the community) are considered in the contingency plans.

Process

- Contingency plans need to be the responsibility of the leader of the department rather than a project team member. This will ensure adequate time is spent creating them and that they are doable. Include explicit instructions on who should activate each plan and when.

- Local examples of how things went wrong in the past are helpful in securing the support and time necessary for building thorough risk analyses. Risks to watch out for include supply to customers, vulnerability to competitors, information interruption, external relations, and employee engagement.

- Develop a consistent template for risk identification and mitigation to help demonstrate that potential problems have been reviewed and planned for (see chart on the next page). An assessment needs to be conducted for each impacted area by members of that group and the project team.

- Ensure that a cross-departmental team with members from all groups operating a process contributes to the contingency plan.

- Spend extra time exploring handovers and interfaces within processes. If you don't, each group could be operating under different assumptions based on current ways of doing things.

- Create a risk analysis to evaluate contingency options (see chart on page 74).

- Establish trigger points to clarify when contingency plans need to be activated. This will speed up remedial actions and minimize damage.

- Review the contingency plans at a leadership team meeting. Leaders must understand potential risks and agree to contingency actions.

Risks are like dormant viruses in that they can erupt at any time and wreak havoc on your project's health. Your project will be more successful if you identify potential risks as early as possible and take preventative steps to avoid them. Once you have done so, you can start thinking about the amount and types of resources you need to implement the change.

Risk Assessment

Key Change: Merged Route to Market	Dimension of Risk	Risk	Mitigating Action	Who	By When
Main Activities	Change leadership and ownership	Misalignment between old and new leaders	Hold leadership meeting to clarify strategy and priorities	Sales leader	January 15
	Resistance				
• Define new route to market for business	Culture	Clashes between cultures	Hold district awareness sessions	District leaders/ project team	March 1
• Define new combined structure	Capacity/ resources	Sales reps poorly trained on new products	Ensure resources and timing for training	Sales trainer	March 1
• Identify and promote advantages of new model	Collaboration/ cooperation				

*http://www.changewithconfidence.com/?page_id=125

Risk Analysis

Risk	Potential Impact	Contingency Option	Impact on Option	Option Selection	Rationale	Criteria for Invoking Contingency	Owner
Sales reps unprepared to sell entire portfolio of products	• Lost distribution • Lower sales • Low margin sales mix • Damaged reputation with customer	• Immediately retrain sales reps	• Increased training and travel costs • Lost sales from time away from customers	✓	• Additional training can be done quickly in regional or district offices, minimizing loss of sales	• Poor product knowledge in change readiness scores • Poor performance during pilot launch	Sales leaders
		• Revert back to two separate sales forces selling legacy product portfolios until year's end • Retrain sales reps at year's end	• Increased administration, training, and travel costs • Lost sales from time away from customers • Damaged reputation with customer	✗	• The old system is working well, although it does not capture benefits from the merger	• Poor product knowledge in change readiness scores • Poor performance during pilot launch	Sales leaders

Resources

CHAPTER 16

How Do I Know What Resources I Need?

Too few people on a project can't solve the problems;
too many create more problems than they solve . . .

—Unknown

Your team will be completing most of the activities on your project plan, and you need to estimate the number of people needed to support the change. Too few resources leads to cut corners, the risk of not being able to adequately manage issues, and burnout. Too many resources tends to create greater complexity, slow reaction time, and cause project delays. Also, you need to ensure your chosen people have the right skills to complete activities. Without change management skills they most likely won't have the necessary influence on stakeholders or the ability to manage tasks. As such, it is critical that you dedicate sufficient time to map out the number and types of team members you need. You also have to fight for required resources at the beginning of a project, as the fight gets harder and more stressful when additional resources are needed midstream. Cutting corners in a budget might look good on paper, but doing so rarely delivers the outcomes you need.

Thumbs Down, Thumbs Up

In the planning phase of a Cadbury Adams USA systems consolidation in 2004, project team members completed a bottom-up analysis of required resources. An estimate was submitted to the leadership team, but only half of the human resources were approved. The change leader shared her concerns with the project manager, outlining the necessary cuts to the training plan and indicating that some areas would now have to deliver their own training (with only minimal support from the project team).

Within six weeks, it was apparent that more resources were required to build people capabilities. The change leader submitted a budget change request, which was approved after intense scrutiny. Training schedules needed to be reworked to fit in additional sessions, and additional costs were incurred for overtime premiums. By cutting people resources, the leadership team assumed that the original budget was inflated. It was not.

Grameen Bank is a micro-finance institution in Bangladesh that extends small unsecured loans to unemployed or low-income entrepreneurs. It operates in almost all of the country's 84,000 rural villages, manages more than 2,500 bank branches, and has over 7.5 million borrowers (97 percent of them women) and over 24,000 employees. It has disbursed $7.6 billion in loans and has a 98-percent repayment rate. The bank is owned by its borrowers, who own 95 percent of its shares (the government owns the remaining 5 percent), and 65 percent of the borrowers have crossed the poverty line. Grameen Bank and its founder, Muhammad Yunus, received the Nobel Peace Prize in 2006.

The bank's strategy and operating model was successful for its first 15 years but proved unstable in 1998, when a flood devastated two-thirds of Bangladesh. For three months the country was in turmoil, and this caused a spike in repayment issues and a liquidity problem because on-time payments dropped to 57 percent. Furthermore, 52 percent of clients stopped making deposits, 95 percent of compulsory savings were withdrawn, and 85 percent of the bank's contingency funds were withdrawn. The problem worsened until 2000, when the bank's leadership decided to reengineer the operating model to provide more flexibility to borrowers. They believed its loan products, policies, and processes were too rigid to deal with seasonal fluctuations or natural disasters.

The second-in-command at the bank was appointed project manager. A central project team was set up to manage issues and share learnings across the branch network. Since the bank was in a high-risk situation, the poorest performing branches needed to return to profitability before the redesign process could begin. Each branch manager was appointed the leader of the change at his or her location, and most staff were invited to participate in the design process. The branch managers documented problems in their areas and provided recommendations to correct them. "SWAT" teams were mobilized to provide extra support to the poorest-performing branches, which became incubators for new ideas. All leaders and most employees were given either input or feedback roles to address resistance to changing ways of working. (The flood was seen by some as a temporary challenge and they longed to return to the prosperity they had experienced before this natural disaster.) Some of these branches had additional challenges because of geographic isolation, so they were selected to pilot the new system. A project manager was appointed to manage the pilot.

The new system needed to be explained to 13,000 staff and the bank's 2.4 million borrowers. A design communications team referred to as the "Coordination and Operation" department was formed to write a guide-book, which included all the rules and regulations for the training program. The department organized a four-day workshop for all managers, some of whom would lead training sessions across the branch network. All 2,539 branches successfully transitioned to the new operating model within 17 months.

What Works

- If your change project includes changes to computer systems, appoint "superusers" for each area. They will ensure that the program meets business needs, as well as help train people on new procedures and coach them through the transition.

- Create a resource plan that identifies the number and type of resources your change project requires. It is helpful to link these requirements to your impact assessment and to document the qualifications required for each role. This resource plan will support discussions with leaders, and trade-off scenarios can be explored if the business can't accommodate your recommendations.

Resource Plan

Resource Type	Number of People Resources	Duration	Stakeholder Management	Process Redesign	Training Design	Training Delivery	Colleague Support
Change Manager	1	6 months	✓	✓	✓		✓
Superuser	0.5	6 months		✓	✓	✓	✓

*http://www.changewithconfidence.com/?page_id=131

- Review past project plans to learn about resourcing levels, and interview the project managers to get their perspectives and advice. (Be careful not to copy someone else's resourcing plan if it doesn't match your needs.)

- Secure enough resources so that you don't compromise stakeholder management. If you're working on the activity-level details, you will be distracted from this important leadership role.

- Research external benchmarks and get advice from third-party partners to test your bottom-up resourcing plan.

- Ensure there is one person responsible for each group impacted by the change. They become the conduits between the business and the project, and become a network of ambassadors across the organization that shares best practices.

- Ideally, get full-time staff resources for your team. If your project involves less than 50 percent of a colleague's time, it will become a secondary priority for him or her. This may not become apparent until you are well into implementation, when it is difficult to renegotiate resourcing agreements.

- Select team members with diverse skills, experiences, tenures, and personalities.

- The resourcing requirements of your project may change as you work through the plan; reinforce with the leadership team that you may need to reallocate resources within your team. This is natural and needs to be communicated to leaders so they don't become overly concerned when you make changes.

Building the right-sized team with the right skills is critical to your change project. It must be large enough to complete planned tasks but not so large that roles overlap and team members become idle. With the right team in place, you can consider what skills are required for you or someone else to manage the project.

CHAPTER 17

What Makes a Good Project Manager?

The most successful project managers have perfected the skill of being comfortable being uncomfortable.

—Unknown

THE PROJECT MANAGER HAS THE GREATEST IMPACT on day-to-day project operations. He or she must have the organizational skills necessary to construct and manage the project plan, be able to uncover missed tasks, have the relationship skills necessary to align and influence diverse stakeholders, and have the critical thinking skills to solve problems. Also, this individual needs to be able to courageously tell the truth and demonstrate grace under pressure in times of difficulty. If you are taking on the project manager role yourself, be sure to build a team that includes the capabilities you don't have. Access to a skill can be as effective as having it yourself, so long as you know when it's needed.

Thumbs Down, Thumbs Up

With 700,000 students and 84,000 employees, the Los Angeles Unified School District (LAUSD) is the second-largest public school system in the United States. In 2007, before a new payroll system was scheduled to be launched, the teachers' union requested that the existing system remain operative. Given the complexity of salary scales, job assignments, and rules, it was concerned that payroll would not run smoothly. Also, numerous red flags had been raised throughout the planning phase of the project that had not been adequately addressed, resulting in the LAUSD's chief information officer resigning six months before the launch. The project team and external consultant group ignored the request and activated the new system as planned.

Tens of thousands of employees were overpaid, underpaid, or not paid at all for months, causing teachers to picket the district school board. The $95-million project ended up costing $210 million (including $6 million in noncollectable overpayments). The project lead had little IT knowledge and no experience of enterprise-wide systems implementations. Under his watch, data wasn't reviewed for accuracy, training of payroll clerks was inadequate, and bugs in the computer system were not fixed. LAUSD officials admitted that the project was too optimistic, didn't recognize (or address) the risks involved, and included improper planning, scheduling, and budgeting.

👍 Cadbury Adams Canada hired a project manager to lead a large systems integration in 2005. This manager had worked on similar assignments as a consultant and came highly recommended. From day one it was clear he had the skills to lead the project. He knew and understood the steps that needed to be taken, managed stakeholders well, and was an expert facilitator of the cross-departmental project team. He demonstrated courage when dealing with regional leaders and had the ability to focus the team on what was most important. He got the right people together to remove barriers and solve problems, and often ended meetings by asking, "How can I help you?"—which set the tone for the project. The leadership team realized the importance of the project manager role and thus hired for experience and skill, which was demonstrated daily.

What Works

- Select someone who:
  - Has the skill set to be successful and who has future potential in the organization. (Running a big change project is an excellent learning experience for a "high-potential" individual.)

- Is an opinion leader in the business and is respected, and whose opinion is sought by others.

- Has past experience working on a project team. This experience is essential to understanding the natural flow of big projects.

- Has a strong informal network across the business. It might take too long to establish credibility with key groups if the chosen project leader (and what he or she has accomplished in the past) is largely unknown.

- Can speak well in front of the leadership team. This person will be presenting updates and needs to be respectful and not afraid to defend decisions or recommend adjustments to the plan.

- Is a good listener, facilitator, negotiator, mediator, and motivator.

• Create an interview guide to ensure structure and consistency in your discussions with candidates. Asking specific questions about their abilities will give you a detailed sense of what they can do, what gaps can be enhanced through coaching, and where other team members will need to step in.

A good project manager is like a modern-day Renaissance man or woman who draws upon strong technical and people skills to maintain momentum regardless of circumstances. They are quick to diffuse concerns and solve problems so that the project does not get bogged down or go off track. With the project manager in place, you can start filling key project roles.

Project Manager Interview Guide

Introduction
- Provide overview of the project
- Give an overview of the role

Capabilities	Question	Response (situation, task, result)	Note
Relationship skills	Could you give me an example of how you have influenced leaders without formal authority?	• Noticed that the top of current packaging was plain and had no branding, unlike our competitors' products • Spoke with brand manager and head of sales • A commercial option was presented and approved • Viewed as a contributing factor to increased sales	• Good problem identification and cross-departmental framing of issue • Partnering for a solution • Tangible results

Close
- Ask candidate if he or she has any questions
- Ask candidate if there is anything else he or she would like to share
- Provide next steps

*http://www.changewithconfidence.com/?page_id=135

CHAPTER 18

How Do I Get the Best People to Join the Project Team?

People will forget what you said, people will forget what you did, but they will never forget how you made them feel.

—Maya Angelou

SELECTING THE BEST TEAM MEMBERS for your project is critical: you need people with the skills, knowledge, and attitude to make a project successful. Once you have identified the profiles you are looking for, your challenge is to sell the benefits of your project to managers of candidates and the leadership team so that they approve your ideal secondments. This done, your role is then to ensure that your project delivers on these benefits by personally monitoring team members' development plans.

There are many reasons why someone *wouldn't* want to be on a project team. He or she might be engrossed in a current role, uninspired by the change, unclear about the fit with career progression, or fearful about finding a good role after the project is completed. You need to present the opportunities and neutralize concerns by promoting the benefits of your project.

Thumbs Down, Thumbs Up

👎 Volvo 3P is the division responsible for product planning, development, and purchasing for all truck companies in the Volvo group. It employs 5,000 people in five continents. In 2006, a study of its project team recruitment process revealed that line managers made all project staffing decisions based on availability, competence, and experience. The absence of project manager input or guidance from the Human Resources department contributed to problems with team dynamics, poor communication, and misalignment of personal and business agendas. One project team member said, "We have little in common in the group, and everyone works on their own goals and agendas."[1] Often the best person for a team was unavailable, leading to poor representation at project meetings, and high turnover resulted in knowledge and experience gaps.

In 2006, Cadbury Adams Canada adopted a new global business decision-making model that included new processes, tools, measurements, and behaviors. The business had just completed a two-year merger, and this was the first major project that didn't focus on integrating the two formerly independent businesses. The leadership team recognized the cultural significance of the project and the importance of modeling new behaviors but realized it needed help adopting them. The team created a new project role, and the person filling it would have to facilitate leadership team meetings, monitor their behaviors, and provide executive coaching. Instead of hiring an external consultant, the team chose an internal business director who had the skills and passion to fulfill the mandate.

To entice the director, the team structured the assignment to broaden her cross-departmental skills. Also, a one-year time frame was established to expedite her return to the business. Furthermore, she was allowed to retain a few business responsibilities from her then-current role to keep her connected to basic operations. She accepted the new role knowing that it was tailored to her needs and aligned with her career path. She performed well and took on more senior roles in the company after the assignment.

What Works

- Create a brand for your project, including an aspirational name. People are drawn to winning teams and want to be attached to exciting projects within an organization.

- Discuss the project with the candidate's department leader and manager before approaching the candidate. You need to understand candidate's development needs and how the project will support him or her.

- Start the conversation with the candidate by outlining your personal views on the project (e.g., what it means to you).

- Discuss how the project work has enhanced your career.

- Reference past projects where people progressed after being on project teams.

- Commit to helping the candidate excel in the project and organization.

People want to do meaningful work, be treated with respect, and be acknowledged for the work they do. The best people demand it. You must present your project as an opportunity to realize these basic human needs. A compelling work environment will attract the best people and retain them. People might forget project details, but they will never forget how it felt to be part of the team.

CHAPTER 19

How Do I Know If a Consultant Can Help Me?

An expert is a man who stopped thinking—he knows!
—**Frank Lloyd Wright**

An ounce of action is worth a ton of theory.
—**Friedrich Engels**

CONSULTANTS CAN BE EXCELLENT PARTNERS to help plan and manage your change project. They can also be lightweight automatons who provide no direction. If you have not managed many change projects, the challenge will be assessing the consultants' depth of experience and abilities. Like most specialist professionals, they come with their own theories, models, and jargon that suggest knowledge, skill, and professionalism. But they can also be experts at masking limited knowledge and inexperience. If you choose the wrong consultant, you'll pay for someone who adds little or no value and, worse, might jeopardize your project.

Another potential hazard is hiring a consultant who has done well on other assignments but doesn't have experience related to your project. Also, while you may be impressed by a lead consultant's experience, his or her team might be made up of people with little germane experience. In this case, you will be paying them to learn their roles—not good value for money.

Thumbs Down, Thumbs Up

In 2004, Marin County, California, hired Deloitte Consulting to implement a new computer system to simplify and automate its Finance and HR business processes. The system did not work as planned. Twenty-six major issues were identified, including the inability to produce financial statements, reconcile cash balances, administer accounts payables and receivables, and access information on pensions. In 2010, the Board of Supervisors voted to abandon the system four years after it went live, and then filed a $30 million lawsuit against the consulting company that designed and installed it. In the Marin County court filing, the board accused Deloitte of winning the contract based on an expert team that was replaced with less experienced and skilled consultants once the contract was signed. The filing read in part:

> Deloitte mounted an extensive sales campaign to be hired by the County. As part of its sales efforts, it repeatedly represented to the county that Deloitte's consultants had the requisite skills and experience to successfully implement a complex ERP software product specifically designed for public service entities . . . [and] had assembled a team of its "best resources" who had "deep SAP and public sector knowledge." These representations were fraudulent. Indeed, at the time Deloitte made them, it knew that it did not have the ability or intention to provide the skilled resources necessary to deliver a successful SAP implementation. Deloitte also knew that because the County did not have any prior ERP implementation or SAP experience in general, or SAP experience in particular, it would be depending on it to oversee, guide, and manage the project . . . rather than providing the County with SAP and public sector expertise, Deloitte used the County's SAP project as a trial-and-error training ground to teach its consultants— many of them neophytes—about SAP for Public Sector software, all at the County's expense.[1]

Deloitte responded to Marin County's filed allegations and issued a statement saying that "[it] denies these inflammatory and false charges and will continue to vigorously defend the case."[2] As of April, 2012, the case was still under review at Marin Superior Court.

👍 One morning in April 2000, employees entering a Cadbury Trebor Allan manufacturing plant were greeted by a man standing on the sidewalk. He said, "hello," gave them each a pamphlet, and encouraged them to read it. The man was from a prominent union, and the pamphlet was an invitation to join. This was a great concern to managers because a union vote would be triggered if 40 percent of the employees signed a card saying they were interested.

Cadbury had always worked well with employee unions—not surprising, as the company operated under the Cadbury family's Quaker belief that all human beings should be treated equally and with respect. The most famous example of their social ethos is Bournville, a utopian village built in 1879 and designed to free workers from the cramped and dirty conditions of inner-city industrial life. In this "factory in a garden," employees owned company-built homes in neighborhoods with gardens, recreational facilities, and public parks to improve their quality of life. Perhaps with this history in mind, the managers took issue with the union drive because they felt they could do a better job of looking after employee needs than a union could, and a third-party organization would only get in the way of doing so.

The Human Resources leader brought in a consultant to deal with this challenge. (This was the consultant's 79th such assignment, of which 77 had been successful and one had not because the client didn't follow his advice.) Within 48 hours he was on site speaking with managers and their team members. He knew how to engage colleagues, have meaningful conversations about needs, and coach managers. Months later, the union vote was averted, and a plan was put in place to address employee concerns. Everyone acknowledged the consultant's contribution and agreed they couldn't have avoided unionization of the site without his leadership.

What Works

- Consider firms or individuals recommended by trusted peers, but do your homework.

- Meet with the consultants (or consultant) who will be doing the work. Some firms have client managers who sell the firm's services but don't actually work on assignments. Also, ensure that all consultants will add value to the change project.

- Ask for the consultants' direct experience in the type of change you are leading, and about the mistakes they have made. (If they claim to have not made any, be suspicious.)

- Ask how they typically spend their time on assignments. If it is spent simply sitting in on regular meetings or developing updates, they will not do much heavy lifting with your team members.

- Test consultants for their ability to be team players. Knowledge is necessary but not sufficient for excellent third-party resources.

- Create an interview guide to assess different consultants, and keep in mind the following:

  - Be wary of references to proprietary methodologies and templates. You need to confirm that the consultant will use approaches and tools appropriate to your project rather than sticking to existing intellectual property that may not fit the need. (I have found that the best consultants use a "toolbox" approach.)

  - Be watchful of a consulting group focused on "getting you out of the gate quickly." Fast is easy; getting the right plans in place to deliver your chosen outcomes takes time.

  - Reserve roles that represent business areas for people who work within the business. No matter how experienced a consultant is, he or she cannot be expected to know the operating details and history of your business and thus fully represent its interests.

A consulting team, or single consultant, can be a powerful asset for your project. Consultants can leverage project management principles to organize and help run your project plan, spot issues before they mushroom into problems, and provide advice on people dynamics. However, you need to ensure that they have the right skills and complement your internal team members. Once you have selected your internal and external team members, you need to get them up to speed.

Consultant Interview Guide

Area	Interview Question	Answer	Comment
Breadth of experience	List the types of change management assignments you have participated in (merger, systems redesign, restructure)?	• Systems upgrade	• No merger experience
Depth of experience	Specifically what roles did you have during each assignment? What were you responsible for?	• Reported to the technical team leader for all assignments	• Very limited interaction with senior stakeholders
Attitude and retrospection/Honesty	Tell me about the biggest mistake you made on a change assignment. What was the impact, and what did you learn?	• Did not communicate a design change to team members, which caused rework and frustration • Now records all changes and highlights them in weekly project updates	• Good understanding of negative consequences and appropriate modification of behavior to avoid repeating the mistake

*http://www.changewithconfidence.com/?page_id=141

CHAPTER 20

How Do I Set Up the Project Team for Success?

The beginning, as the proverb says, is half the whole.
—Aristotle

HOW YOU SET UP THE PROJECT TEAM will set the tone of the project and communicate how you will run it. The kickoff meeting is a golden opportunity to demonstrate your leadership style and establish guidelines for behaviors so that team members work well together, avoid barriers, and manage conflicts.

The first step is to define the work environment you believe will enable your team. Typically, collaborative, committed, hard-working, and fun environments are the most effective. These characteristics need to be portrayed in your kickoff meeting, and by modeling these behaviors, your team members will follow suit.

Big change projects are generally very stressful, so permission to be humorous, even silly, in certain situations can lead to more energized, focused, and effective team members. Humor is an escape valve, and there are just too many tragic examples of team members not having this outlet and who, as a result, crumbled under the strain of having to deliver. It is the project manager's role to keep his or her team from melting down. There is no excuse for burning out your team. Don't do it.

Thumbs Down, Thumbs Up

👎 In 2002, Cadbury Schweppes became the world's largest confectionery company when it bought Adams for $4.2 billion. The merger was the biggest it had ever managed, and it was closely watched by financial analysts because some thought the price paid was too high. A successful integration was necessary for good financial performance and investor confidence. There was a lot on the line.

The U.S. project kickoff meeting focused on the magnitude of the change that needed to be made, and the executive sponsor and project manager reinforced the steepness of the mountain the team was about to climb. The executive sponsor ended the meeting by asking the team, given the enormous task ahead of them, who felt confident. The answers confirmed that people were consumed by the enormity of the task and were preoccupied with the "Long and Winding Road" positioning (rather than "We Are the Champions"). After the short meeting ended, everyone left quietly, absorbed in his or her own reflections. Focusing on the difficulties ahead was like kryptonite to Superman. It drained people of energy and confidence, making room for fear and insecurity.

👍 With a user group of 40,000 employees worldwide, Cisco Systems, a $43-billion technology company that designs, manufactures, and sells networking equipment, started the biggest IP telephony project (data, voice, and video that are transmitted over one network system) in history. A cross-departmental team was set up based on the skills and technical expertise required, and representation came from all locations of the corporation. The team kicked off the project by discussing the benefits of the new network, and ensured that all team members bought into the need for the change. The team then discussed team structure and collaboration, communication needs, employee requirements, and, finally, drafted a vision that the executive sponsor (the CEO) supported and shared with the organization. Roles and responsibilities were discussed and agreed upon, and each group talked about the value it brought to the project.

The cross-departmental team created guidelines to ensure its members worked well together, including a commitment to open and honest communication, transparency vis-à-vis calendars and schedules, and the documentation of changes made by subteams. Weekly meetings were scheduled to give updates, discuss issues, and share accomplishments. Key messages were communicated by the team and the steering committee to ensure that everyone associated with the project would consistently speak about it. They also reviewed team feedback from an employee survey about "must-have" features of the new system so that all subteams were working with the same understanding of what was important to employees about the new system's features. The project was successfully completed on time in 2003.

What Works

- Hold a project kickoff meeting as soon as the project team is formed. This will allow you to brief team members on project details, build excitement about the experience, answer any questions, and start to develop new relationships.

- Start the meeting by providing an outline of the business need and how the project will address it, and close with guidelines on how the team wants to work together.

Kickoff Meeting Agenda

Agenda
Warm-up introduction exercise
Executive sponsor/project manager opening (thank you)
Project overview
– Rationale for the project
– Objectives
– Outcomes/deliverables (and measurements)
– High-level overview of plan
– Team structure and "What's in it for me?"
Exercise: Project enablers and challenges
Exercise: Team ground rules
Closing comments

*http://www.changewithconfidence.com/?page_id=145

- Ensure that all team members attend this meeting, even if you have to delay it to accommodate schedules.

- Invite the executive sponsor to open the session, to demonstrate high-level support and strategic alignment.

- Infuse passion about the project into your brief; for example, "This is a once in a lifetime opportunity . . . " or "This is the first time in our company's history . . . " or "We are the first national division or department to take on this challenge . . . "

- Share what the project means to you and how it will benefit the team.

- Present the key communications messages about the project and gain feedback on them:

  – Why is the project necessary for the long-term health of the organization?

  – What will it do?

  – What needs to change?

  – How will people be involved in the planning and transition stages?

  – What will happen and when?

- Ask team members to share past experiences that will contribute to the project's success. (Often people's past experiences are either unknown or ignored.)

- Build in time for the team members to interact and get to know each other. Great work comes from groups that have made personal connections and have developed an appreciation for past experiences, skills, and accomplishments.

- Record all questions and ensure that the ones that have not been answered are followed up on. The diligence involved in answering questions reinforces expectations about honoring personal commitments.

Environment

- Secure a space for your project team to work together. This will facilitate dialogue and speed up decision making.

- Develop ground rules for the team—the more interactive and cocreated, the better. People are more likely to follow rules they create.

- Avoid military symbolism like "war room" or "command center." Many projects use such terms because they communicate hierarchy and urgency. However, they also encourage command-and-control behaviors such as leader-only decision making and selective communication of information, and can play on fear and intimidation, which destroy productivity.

- Hold weekly team alignment meetings where updates from all areas are shared. Brief progress summaries will ensure everyone receives the latest information.

- Keep formal documentation to a minimum. It is easy to overdocument, causing your team to spend more time on paperwork than helping people make the change.

Data

- Accurate data is critical to a successful change project. If it is not available, develop a process to gather it and assign resources to do so.

- Create a factbook summarizing all critical data that needs to be tracked for the project. This will give you an accurate baseline to share with stakeholders and a source of reference for all of the performance indicators you are tracking.

It is important to motivate team members before they dive into the project. Setting a positive and productive tone will enable them to work together and optimize their capabilities. Skipping this step leads to an extended ramp-up time, miscommunication, and stress. By effectively managing the front end of a project, you will eliminate many of the barriers that can slow down a new team. This holds true for leadership teams and senior advisors, who also need to be fully engaged and committed to the project.

Communication

CHAPTER 21

How Do I Get Leaders to Personally Commit to the Project?

While the mind looks for proof, the heart looks for engagement.
While the mind looks for information, the heart looks for passion.
—**Terry Pearce**

Indifference and neglect often do much more damage
than outright dislike.
—**J.K. Rowling**

LEADERS CAN MAKE OR BREAK a big change project. Given the power of their positions, they can reward the behaviors and actions they support and punish those they don't. Without their full support, a project has little chance of succeeding.

People will emulate leaders' behaviors, believing they have silent permission to parrot actions demonstrated at the top of the power hierarchy. Leaders' lack of visible commitment, reluctance to adopt new behaviors, and/or poor attendance at project review meetings will result in similar actions from their teams. Conversely, aligned, energized, and fully supportive leaders will motivate and galvanize their teams to adopt new ways of working and endure difficult transitions.

Thumbs Down, Thumbs Up

👎 In 1999, the U.S. Internal Revenue Service embarked on a 15-year, $8-billion change project to modernize its IT systems and business applications. It was a risky endeavor because the master data file being updated contained the last 40 years' worth of tax records of over 227 million individuals and corporations. By 2004, the project had experienced many delays, with cost overruns of nearly $300 million. One of the main shortfalls was leadership engagement. The leadership team failed to create a consistent long-term vision for the project, did not have assigned responsibilities, and did not insist on a process for evaluating progress. The team members were often absent from project meetings and did not provide technical leadership for the project, demonstrating that they did not support the initiative. In 2006, the project was recast with a smaller scope and budget. In 2010, after a $3.7-billion investment, some software programs had been launched, but they either did not work as intended or had security vulnerabilities.

👍 A president of Cadbury Adams Canada showed his support for a new global strategy development process in 2005 by enrolling all of his senior and midlevel managers in a four-day training program. As requested, he also signed up his entire leadership team to participate in case-study role plays.

This leader made the ultimate commitment to the program when he accepted a request from the global head office, which was looking for a national leadership team to film business strategy dialogue using behaviors prescribed in the training. The video would be played and analyzed at a global conference attended by the top 150 leaders, including the chief executive and chairman. Not only did the leader agree to have the dialogue filmed, he insisted that no edits be made. He wanted to demonstrate both good and poor behaviors and give permission to his team to try new practices.

The video captured behavior of his that was not aligned with the new ways of working, and he asked for that clip to also be shown at all local training sessions. His example demonstrated that leaders needed to change too, and only through courageous practice would new ways of working be adopted. If he could do it, so could they.

What Works

Positioning

- Appeal to the rational and emotional motivations of leaders—their hearts and minds. Personal commitment intensifies when they establish emotional attachments with the change project. You need to spell out why these people should care. (For example, it could be because of an emotional reaction to a competitor beating your organization in the marketplace.) The more connections you raise, the more likely one will resonate with your stakeholders.

- Establish a common goal that all members will benefit from.

- Link the project with a leader's personal success. Being the best among your peers is a powerful motivator.

- Limit your project's duration to one year. Objectives should be set annually, as multiyear projects risk priorities changing and support being withdrawn, causing the project to stall. Also, leaders typically are more engaged in projects that start and finish before they move on to their next roles, as they are responsible for outcomes. Break multiyear projects into multiple one-year initiatives.

- When you do get agreement from the leadership team members, thank them for their support and reinforce that the project is owned by all members of the team.

Participation

- Compare your leaders to other industry leaders recognized for championing similar projects. Quoting recognized sources like the *Harvard Business Review* can help crystallize these comparisons.

- Get the head of the organization to commit to your change project, and have him or her share with the leadership team members the reasons why he or she did so.

- Establish roles for leaders that keep them busy and visible. Keep them active on your project.

- Share your project planning process with leadership team members and invite them to evaluate it.

- Get the leadership team members to buy into you. Business is personal and people want to be associated with (and to help) those they have a personal connection with.

Leadership team member commitment is a requirement for change success. Commitment is a very human thing, and you need to find the right motivations for them to personally invest in your project. Once you do, it's up to you, your team, and leaders to help colleagues successfully manage their teams through the change.

CHAPTER 22

How Can I Help Leaders Prepare
for Their Roles?

During highly charged times of transition, everything takes
on a symbolic hue—everything means something.
—William and Susan Bridges

LEADERSHIP IS ABOUT SETTING A DESTINATION and marshaling resources to get there. Leadership roles can change throughout the phases of your project—from builder of awareness and agreement, to thought leadership and resource provider, to motivator and remover of barriers, to reinforcer and rewarder. Often, leaders are unclear of the project roles they are required to play, usually because they are unaware of the details of the project, and therefore can say or do things that appear inappropriate. It is your role to thoroughly brief and monitor leaders to keep them aligned with the goals of the project.

For big change projects, leaders need to model the new behaviors that will enable the change. If they are not the first to make changes, colleagues will be less willing to do so. You need to coach leaders on how to demonstrate new ways of working and provide candid feedback when they don't.

Thumbs Down, Thumbs Up

During the demerger of the Cadbury Schweppes beverages and confectionery divisions in 2007, there was speculation by IT colleagues about which company would be better to work for. The beverages side, called Dr Pepper Snapple Group, had an emotional advantage in that the head office was located in Dallas, where the Dr Pepper brand was king. Cadbury Chocolate was a small brand in the United States that was dwarfed by the "23 authentic flavors" heavyweight. Also, everyone knew that the Cadbury employees would be leaving palatial offices for a less well-appointed location in 2007.

The communications and change teams worked hard to present both companies as equal employment opportunities. At an all-employees meeting, a senior leader of the beverages division described how "we" were all Dr Pepper Snapple Group employees and how proud "we" should be to be part of the team. Those who knew they would be staying with Cadbury were crestfallen. The project team went into damage control mode, reinforcing the key message of building two great companies. In times of change, executives can become divorced from the realities (and anxieties) faced by colleagues. Their inappropriate actions (although unintentional) send shockwaves through an organization that will create rumors and dissonance. You need to move quickly to reinforce key messages and take steps to make sure disruptions don't arise or are not repeated.

Saudi Aramco is the largest exporter of oil and natural gas in the world—and its largest private company. In 2011, the president and CEO announced a $1.25-billion change project to transform the company into "the world's leading integrated energy and chemicals company" by 2020.

Before the program was launched, leaders participated in a strategic business review to identify challenges and helpful industry-wide trends, and concluded that Saudi Aramco's culture would have to significantly change to manage a more global, diversified, and technology-based business. They realized the next generation of leaders would be from Generation Y, as nearly 40 percent of Aramco's employees around the world were under age 30. This group needed a stimulating, challenging, and inclusive work environment to unlock its potential, instead of the current "command and control" management style. The leaders' roles shifted from telling employees what to do to fostering environments for their teams to succeed (including instilling company values, work ethic, and standards). They were given training on how to be more empowering and were rewarded for decentralizing decision making and participating in a new mentoring program to provide broader leadership exposure and guidance. The leaders were supported by a new internal communications strategy that included social media tools to appeal to technology-savvy employees, and feedback from a new Young Leaders Advisory Board on how to incorporate ideas and insights into the transformation project. In addition to this support, the compensation structure was aligned with the new roles to ensure the new leader behaviors were rewarded.

What Works

- Help leaders understand that everything they do and say related to the project impacts colleagues' perceptions of it.

- Provide feedback immediately after a leader has presented at an employee meeting. Track his or her behaviors and point out when they are not appropriate.

- Review leadership roles in person, either one on one or with the full leadership team. Discuss how the new behaviors manifest themselves in real-life situations. Supporting leadership decisions means that a leader must publicly support a decision even if he or she disagrees with it.

- Create a one-page leader role summary. It can be reviewed in coaching sessions to acknowledge aligned behaviors and pinpoint gaps.

- Book weekly one-hour meetings with each leader. The meetings can be shorter if there is nothing to discuss, but they should be prebooked for the duration of the project.

It is your role to prepare leaders for their roles in the project. Awareness, skill building, feedback, and coaching can build them into the role models you require to encourage change. Helping them create a picture of the future is another way you can help them be successful.

Leader Role Summary

Area	Responsibility	Specifics
Governance	Direct the project according to guiding principles	• Attend project status updates • Provide advice and support • Make decisions based on project status
Behaviors	Actively demonstrate the behaviors that enable the project's outcomes	• Visibly support leadership decisions • Actively participate in meetings • Integrate new behaviors in day-to-day management activities
Communication	Represent the project and deliver communication messages	• Reinforce benefits • Brief teams on updates and requirements • Share team wins

*http://www.changewithconfidence.com/?page_id=151

CHAPTER 23

How Do I Describe the Better Future My Project Will Bring?

When one is addressing a diverse or heterogeneous audience, the story must be simple . . . emotionally resonant, and evocative of positive experience.

—Howard Gardner

PEOPLE NEED TO KNOW how your project will contribute to a better future. They will ask, "How does this change make the organization better?" and "How will it make my life better?" If you don't answer these questions, many colleagues will resist taking on new ways of working. You must nail "the vision thing."

The best future visions appeal to the hearts and minds of colleagues. Winning over hearts ensures personal investment and engagement; winning over minds ensures alignment with the need for change from a business perspective. Individuals need to see themselves having roles in the future picture you create, and the company rewards for creating change need to be seen as their rewards.

Thumbs Down, Thumbs Up

Farina Group is a 70-store luxury goods retailer in China. The leadership team decided to purchase a new IT system even though the existing systems were working well. They decided to change computer systems because most of Farina Group's competitors had purchased the same system and suppliers had repeatedly met with them, lauding the benefits they were missing. The executive team decided to treat the project as a technical initiative and not upgrade their core processes at the time of installation or communicate the benefits of the new system to employees. They also delegated the project to the IT department without any participation from other departments. In 2003, shortly after the project began, the project leader left the business because of tensions with multiple departments, requiring the head of IT to assume the role. Two stores tested the new system and found it did not meet many of their requirements. Adjustments were made, but more technical problems were identified, resulting in more and more "fixes." Stores continued using the existing systems after the company-wide launch, and the new system was eventually abandoned.

Employing nearly 225,000 people, the State Bank of India (SBI) is the leading commercial bank in that country. When a new chairman took over in 2006, the state-owned bank had been losing market share for two decades. It had missed out on two new financial products opportunities, and its staff was lethargic. Most importantly, the bank appeared to have lost its sense of purpose. From its creation in 1955, SBI was an influential force in economic, industry, and government circles. It played a key role in modernizing the agricultural sector, growing industry, and supporting infrastructure (especially in rural areas). By 2006, however, SBI was just another bank competing against private Indian banks and foreign competitors.

The chairman began by meeting with small groups of senior leaders, aligning them on issues and outlining opportunities. Then he met for five days with his 25 most senior leaders. His presentation opened with a showing of *The Legend of Bagger Vance*, a movie about a golfer who loses but then regains his swing. He created context for the movie by referencing traditional Indian texts like the *Bhagavad Gita*, which teaches "that karma and excellence can be their own reward," drawing parallels between this story and regaining business success and relevance. The rest of the meeting was spent building a 14-point agenda that was given to the 10,000 branch managers during public meetings. These meetings included open forums for colleagues to share their perceptions and to make suggestions. A two-day program was launched called "Parivartan" (transformation) to build awareness for the need for change and to reinforce the chairman's vision for the future. These meetings preempted all other training. At the end of the chairman's five-year term, the State Bank had regained its prominence in India's financial community.

What Works

Content

- Establish a connection between your change project's vision and your organization's overall strategy. This will provide credibility for your initiative.

- Discuss how the change will impact customers, consumers, suppliers, government, and the community.

- Communicate through stories and metaphors. People learn through simple narratives around goals, challenges, actions, and outcomes.

- Share stories about other companies that faced similar challenges, what they did to manage them, and the benefits they gained from doing so.

- Include videos of leaders talking about their challenges.

- If people will be losing things, give them a chance to grieve. Until you do this, people will not fully move away from the present toward the intended future. Also, position your change project as the best option available. Staff can handle the truth but not surprises.

Process

- The more you can encourage people to comment on your vision, the more you will understand the spectrum of opinions about it.

- Give everyone a role in achieving the vision, including articulating things they must do for the change to be successful—for example, attend training or switch to new templates.

- Thank people in advance for their support and contributions.

A vision of a better future provides a common goal for people to identify with and work toward. Once established, a vision becomes a touchstone for reminding them why they are enduring hardships as they take on new ways of working. Once people understand where your change project will take them, you need to secure their sustained commitment.

CHAPTER 24

How Do I Get People to Care about My Project?

Ultimately, people change from the "inside out," not by force from the outside in. People change when they choose to change.
—Linda Ackerman Anderson and Dean Anderson

Inspiring people to action is one thing; helping them sustain this over time is much more difficult.
—James G. Bohn

A SUCCESSFUL VISION creates excitement and interest around things to come, but the level of intensity will decrease—often dramatically so—if you do not maintain momentum. You need to keep your vision top-of-mind at your organization and make it easy for colleagues to transition successfully.

Generally, sustaining change requires people to be personally committed to the project. These connections build emotional bonds that encourage supportive behaviors like spotting barriers and attending training. The easiest and most effective way to build these connections is through opportunities to participate, and the more you ask people to help design and implement the change, the better.

When people care about a project, they are more willing to try new ways of working. Often the harder challenge, however, is for people to give up time-honored practices. People are creatures of habit, and it's human nature for them to hold onto things they value *and* to assume the worst if they are taken away. Many established practices have been cocreated by colleagues, have led to past successes, or have become easy to do. Why should they give them up? Colleagues need to care more about your project and the benefits it offers than they do their current ways of working for them to willingly change.

Thumbs Down, Thumbs Up

FoxMeyers Drugs was a $5 billion pharmaceuticals distribution company, the fourth largest in the United States. It filed for bankruptcy in 1996 after a failed warehouse systems implementation compromised its ability to ship. The CEO had positioned the project as a $40 million cost-cutting initiative that would allow the company to consolidate inventory and close three warehouses. Warehouse employee commitment to the project (and morale) was low, and, after the system was activated, bitter employees failed to fill orders and damaged inventory being shipped, resulting in losses of $34 million. On top of this, many employees quit during the transition, leaving the three facilities understaffed and unprepared (and unwilling) to manage the change.

In 2002, Cadbury Chocolate Canada initiated a productivity improvement project. Before it was launched, colleagues were interviewed and asked why they liked working for the company. The most common answers were "the people" and "the products." A video was created of these responses that played at town hall meetings before the president announced the new project. It was called "Brand New: The Best." He encouraged colleagues to be the best in everything they did and made a connection between his request and the pride they already felt in the company. Leveraging sources of pride helped colleagues find meaning in the project and "The Best" motto became a symbol of employee pride and a rallying cry for improvement.

What Works

Content

- Ensure that your main message is clear, simple, and easy to share—something that can be expressed in fewer than 15 words.

- Give people examples of what they will be able to do in the future that they can't do now. This can lead to future bragging rights to their family and friends.

- Make it personal. Share stories that colleagues can relate to and use examples they have shared with you. Also, informally mingle with employees before you address them. Most leaders don't, and when they do, people will notice.

- Share examples of how specific leaders have demonstrated the new behaviors. If it is good enough for the leaders, it will be good enough for those who respect them.

- Be specific about what you need from colleagues. Keep these requirements to a few things such as attending training and providing feedback on how the transition is going.

Process

- Managers influence how their team members view change. Provide them with fact sheets and Q&A documents to help them answer questions and manage objections.

- Get people's attention by approaching employees in ways different from in the past. For example, if town hall meetings have always been held in auditoriums, hold them in the parking lot. If only the CEO has presented, have the project team do most of the presenting.

- Give employees time to consider the changes, opportunities to ask questions, and ways of providing feedback. They may provide insights that the team is unaware of.

- Create a feedback committee composed of a representative from each impacted group, and respond to questions within 48 hours.

- Keep your promises. Colleagues note and track leadership commitments and will lower their engagement levels (and expectations) if commitments are not realized.

- Make a symbolic change at the beginning of the project, such as no meetings on Friday afternoons. Small but visible changes will be recognized and discussed.

- Make heroes out of people who are driving the project or adopting the change.

- Win over influencers first—the people who are respected and listened to.

- Build energy and excitement throughout the project. What is the new news that will create a buzz? What unexpected results will get people excited?

People make change, and the more they care about your project, the greater the effort they will give to making it successful. It is difficult for most people to change how they work, and you need to create an environment where they can participate and develop personal bonds that will remind them of the importance of making the changes. Commitment is necessary but not sufficient. You also have to help them get through the difficult process of changing.

CHAPTER 25

How Do I Make My Project the Highest Priority?

A terrible thing happens when you don't promote yourself . . . nothing.

—**P.T. Barnum**

Always design a thing by considering it in its next larger context—a chair in a room, a room in a house, a house in an environment, an environment in a city plan.

—**Eliel Saarinen**

THERE IS A TENDENCY FOR CHANGE LEADERS to dive into the details of their project before surveying the business environment in which their project will operate. It is almost inevitable that other projects are either underway or being planned as you start your change project, and thus you will have to compete for resources, communications, leadership, and colleague attention. Unless you make your project stand out, other, better-funded or -promoted projects will get attention; yours won't.

Thumbs Down, Thumbs Up

Global Sales at Cadbury decided to build a sales training academy in 2008. For years, every national division had created its own training programs based on local needs, and there was little sharing of training materials. (Some programs had been designed by the same consultants using similar material, but each national division had paid full design costs.)

The first step of the project was to summarize and catalogue existing training programs used around the world. Local businesses would then be able to select programs from a broader menu based on their needs. Briefing sessions about the initiative were held with local sales training managers, followed by a request for copies of their training materials. Submissions were received by all regions except the one that had invested the most in training design. Follow-up calls and emails to the sales director and his head of training were unsuccessful. As months went by, new global sales projects were launched that were of greater interest to the local businesses than training optimization. Interest in the project dropped until it was put on hold. It was never reinstated. Since it wasn't a priority for *all* national division sales leaders, there was little support to drive action—the death knell for the global sales training academy.

👍 A Cadbury Trebor Allan brand manager was given the challenging task of increasing sales on the underperforming Jersey Milk chocolate bar. It hadn't been promoted in years and had little traction with consumers. He started his task with a small budget and little support.

He researched the Jersey Milk brand and discovered it was celebrating its 75th anniversary the following year. After finding the original artwork in the company archives, he had what he needed to build a consumer story around the product's heritage. He approached the sales leadership team and made the case that customers would be interested in a nostalgic product, an argument he backed up with industry examples. Also, he demonstrated how the sales team could profile the product with little investment. His marketing budget would cover the new classic packaging, and the communications team agreed to provide public relations support.

Once he got approval to launch the Jersey Milk promotion, he spent time with the sales representatives in stores and attended all district and regional team meetings. He showed confidence in the sales team and gave them a program that was easy to implement. Sales grew exponentially and at a higher rate than better-funded chocolate brands, and his product was now on the company's radar. He attributed its success to the sales team that had believed in his vision.

The brand manager was successful because he raised the profile of his project by giving the organization a reason to believe. He also made it easy to support his project and gave credit to others. It was no surprise when his next project was successful, too.

What Works

- Measure your success based on external benchmarks. Comparing your organization to the best of your competitors and other lauded organizations is a good way to intensify focus and gain attention.

- Attract the attention of key people in senior management. Their mention of your project will raise its profile.

- Present an overview of your project at all department team meetings.

- Strive to get the most talented colleagues on your team. Their involvement will suggest that your change project is important.

- Ask the leader of the company to be the executive sponsor. People will notice his or her involvement.

- Communicate more than other project teams are communicating. Spending time updating colleagues on developments will send a message that your project is on the radar and successful.

In a world of constant change and limited budgets, your project is in competition for the resources required for success. You must raise its profile so it secures and maintains leader and colleague attention. One of the ways to do so is through powerful communications that build awareness, interest, and support.

CHAPTER 26

How Do I Communicate to the Organization?

Electric communication will never be a substitute for the face of someone who with their soul encourages another person to be brave and true.

—Charles Dickens

COMMUNICATION SETS THE TONE for the project, provides knowledge to individuals, and reinforces behaviors that support the change deemed necessary. When done well, the results are brilliant; when done poorly, it leads to unclear messaging, incorrect perceptions, and disenfranchised employees.

Communicating well about a project is difficult, although it can appear easy. Colleagues have different communication preferences (from visual to audio to kinesthetic), but generally only a fraction of messages register when they are received. If you don't offer messages in multiple formats, repeated many times, you run the risk that they will be heard by only a portion of your team. Even then, measuring the effectiveness of your communications approach is hard to do in an accurate and timely manner.

Inconsistency of messages is a common problem with change communications. It leads to misinformation, confusion, and colleague indifference. Investment is required to ensure your communications are aligned, and a detailed communications plan is the best tool for getting the right information to the right people at the right times. Well-informed and energized colleagues are best positioned to adopt new ways of working and to realize the benefits from your change project.

Thumbs Down, Thumbs Up

👎 In 2010, at the start of the Kraft Cadbury merger, the initial communications were excellent. A reputable external communications partner was engaged, a website set up to share information, and regular updates were given globally, regionally, and locally. As a new Kraft Foods employee, I was impressed. After the 90-day mark, however, when many of the integration commitments had been successfully implemented, the level of communication dropped to almost nothing. The sudden quietness made many people feel they were uninformed and out of touch. Also, some colleagues felt this was a sign of the integration becoming a secondary priority.

Ironically, if the initial communications hadn't been so good, the drop wouldn't have been as noticeable. Colleagues need consistent and timely information, especially when they feel they have little control. Stories of early merger successes and testimonials about the benefits realized would have filled the communications void. Every change carries a message, and in terms of communication, less is never more.

👍 The project team created a two-phased communications plan to support the integration of Cadbury Chocolate Canada and Trebor Allan. This was the first acquisition in Canada after the U.K.-based Cadbury Schweppes repurchased the Canadian Cadbury business in 1996. A similar merger had been completed in the United Kingdom a few years before, and this heightened the interest of the parent company.

The first phase's objectives were to minimize risk, retain and reengage colleagues, and eliminate barriers to integration. The second phase's objectives were to maintain consistent and timely communications, manage people through change, retain and reengage colleagues, and build a new culture to support business goals. Initiatives were tailored to these objectives and executed over an 18-month period. At this time, the two organizations (and cultures) successfully integrated into one with almost no loss of talent. The plan won an International Association of Business Communicators award for excellence because the communications were tied to project objectives, paralleled the phases of transition, and were planned and delivered consistently throughout the duration of the project.

What Works

Content

- Start the conversation with colleagues with facts: Why do we need to change?

- Ensure you communicate basic information about the project early on:
  - Why is the project necessary for the long-term health of the organization?
  - Why is it achievable?
  - What will it do?
  - What needs to change and what needs to stay as is?
  - How will it be good for you?
  - How will people be involved in the planning and transition stages?
  - What support (training, coaching, practice sessions, etc.) will colleagues be given to help them take on new ways of working?
  - What will happen and when?

- Be transparent with your communications—people can accept the truth, but not surprises or mistruths. Once you lose credibility, it is generally lost for good.

- Admit that the transition will not be perfect and that some things will go wrong. This raises awareness that making mistakes is natural to all transitions and that embedding change takes time.

- Outline expectations of employees, including old behaviors and approaches that need to end.

- Continually remind colleagues that the change is necessary, especially when they are giving up things they know for things they don't know.

- Communicate that not all details have been worked out and that colleagues' input is welcome and needed. This will increase their level of participation and sense of control.

- Always preview the next phase and key dates of the project so there are no surprises (and no knee-jerk reactions).

Leadership

- Keep leaders' messages simple and concise so that they are easy to understand and repeatable.

- Ensure the messages are phrased in the style of the leader. If not, the delivery will seem scripted, perhaps even insincere.

- Brief managers on major announcements before briefing their teams. The managers will be expected to answer questions and must be prepared to be credible sources of information.

Process

- Use all available channels (e.g., meetings, print, email, intranet, etc.), especially those that are the most popular with colleagues.

- Create two-way communication opportunities; they are essential to engaging individuals and understanding their current perceptions. Live updates at the group-wide and working-team levels enable individuals to internalize how the change will impact them.

- Ensure you hold town hall sessions at every location, including manufacturing and warehouse sites.

- Develop a thorough and thoughtful communications plan (see chart on the next page). It will help you align stakeholders with your communications strategy and their roles in delivering it.

- Validate the communications plan against the project plan to ensure that communications requirements have not been missed.

Communications Plan

WHEN? Target Date	WHAT? Key Message	WHO? Communicator(s)	WHY? Objective	HOW? Method
May 1	• We are making changes so that we can better serve customers • We are progressing well • We need colleagues' support to successfully adopt these changes	• President • Leadership team members	• Reinforce commitment to the change project • Share early wins • Encourage colleague engagement with the project	• Town hall presentations • President's blog

*http://www.changewithconfidence.com/?page_id=161

- Give employees a visual representation of what the new environment will look like—a day in the life—and spell out what will change (roles, structure, systems, process, skills, mind-sets, and behaviors).

- Use the branding elements of the project (motivational project name, logo, and tagline) in all communications.

- Identify a communications point person for every group in the organization, even those that are not affected. Brief them on the key messages and communications before they are released.

- Ask a sample set of colleagues to review the communications going to their groups. This will increase the likelihood that they are understood and well received.

- Hold weekly communications review meetings—what has been communicated, how was it received, what was the feedback, what are the lessons learned, what needs to be communicated next week.

- Communicate relevant updates to external partners, including customers, suppliers, and community organizations.

Effective project communications provide relevant and timely information to all stakeholders so that everyone has a consistent understanding of the purpose, requirements, and progress of your change project. Investing the time in creating a detailed communications plan will help people do what you need them to do when you need them to do it.

Now that you have completed the "Planning for Change" phase, you are ready to start managing the project.

PART 3

Managing Change

ONCE YOU'VE CREATED YOUR PLAN and it's been approved, you need to take action as quickly as possible. Ideally, you will implement your plan as it has been written, completing each activity and achieving each milestone on schedule. What typically happens, however, is that roadblocks appear along the way, changing timelines and the sequence of events. You will need to marshal your resources to address these challenges, while managing stakeholders to ensure they remain supportive of the project and your leadership. You'll need to ensure your team has the resources it needs, inform and coach stakeholders, and resolve issues.

The Plan

CHAPTER 27

How Do I Manage My Day Job, Change Project, and Life?

The most basic rule of time management is do the most important things first.
—**Edwin C. Bliss**

IT'S ESSENTIAL FOR YOUR PHYSICAL AND MENTAL HEALTH to recognize that you are moving into a high-performance period, marked by long hours and conflicting priorities. Big change projects will eat up as much time as is available in your schedule, and unless you make room for the other parts of your life, including family and your regular job, they will suffer.

High-performance individuals usually fall into the trap of trying to do everything (while not dropping any balls), and either fail to do so over time or maintain everything poorly. They find it hard to focus on the task at hand because they are so distracted by everything else they must do. Usually, those who work around the clock with no breaks for personal priorities lose perspective because they no longer see the big picture. Leaders who successfully balance their many life roles, in contrast, tend to develop mechanisms to keep on track. Although each one is different, they hardwire priorities into their schedules and ensure that the important things in their lives are honored and done first. This is the way they operate, and they don't apologize for it.

Thumbs Down, Thumbs Up

👎 In 1984, a leader at Château-Gai Wines was a high achiever. He always proclaimed that he had given up everything for the company. As Château-Gai embarked on an aggressive retail expansion initiative, some board members noticed that he looked worn out and worried that his schedule was affecting his decision-making abilities. They counseled him to take time off, which he agreed to do but didn't. The next time the board members spoke with him, they assigned him a maximum number of work hours per week and told him that if he didn't follow their instructions he would be removed from his position. Six months later, he was removed from his position. Capacity is a big issue with big change projects. At a certain point, giving more produces less. In extreme cases, losing perspective can lead to losing your job.

👍 A Cadbury leader viewed Monday to Friday as company time, and at 5 p.m. on Friday, she shut off her BlackBerry until early Monday morning, when she responded to weekend messages. Certain key people had her personal mobile phone number for emergencies, which were rare. This schedule kept her productive and full of energy.

👍 An American Express Sales leader was constantly on the road visiting the regions that reported to him but never missed one of his son's football games. He did whatever it took to be home on game days, including rescheduling meetings and traveling through the night. As he told a Strategic Account Management Association conference audience: "This is one of my greatest achievements."

👍 A commercial leader joined Cadbury during a major transformation. She was an effervescent and engaging person who worked long hours to get up to speed and manage her role. She also went home every night to have dinner with her family (unless on the road or at a business dinner). It was fascinating watching how regimented she was in leaving the office in order to live up to her personal commitments. It is important to understand your personal priorities when working on a big change project: you must manage both work and personal needs.

What Works

- Assign many of your day job tasks to team members as soon as you are assigned to lead a big change project. If you don't have a team, meet with your manager to redistribute this work. You need to have faith that it can and will be done by others.

- Lead the project by delegating most tasks within the project plan to your team. This will free you up to manage the overall project, especially to coach stakeholders.

- Create a to-do list with all of the different aspects of your life—change project, day job, family, self, community, and so on—represented. Devoting time every week to each area will give you a sense of balance.

- Give yourself small rewards related to your hobbies or interests. Time these awards with the successful completion of project milestones.

- Be selective about the meetings you attend. Consider sending a team member to represent you if there's not a specific reason for you to be there.

Priority Grid

WORK (Change Project)
- Attend weekly sponsor update meetings
- Attend all leadership team meetings

FAMILY AND FRIENDS
- Attend final concerts/games
- Be home for birthdays and anniversary
- Arrive home on Friday nights at 6 p.m.

HEALTH
- Exercise three times per week
- Have an annual physical

WORK (Day Job)
- Keep mentoring commitments
- Attend biweekly team meetings

COMMUNITY
- Attend school council meetings

*http://www.changewithconfidence.com/?page_id=184

- Share your priority list with your manager, team, and family so that people don't have misguided expectations.

- Create a priority grid of nonnegotiable commitments you intend to keep. They will be challenged when you get into the middle of project management, so put them in writing before project dates are set.

Change leaders need to plan their schedules as rigorously as their change projects. Determining your priorities in all aspects of your life will enable you to be balanced, even when you have less time to dedicate to each element. If done well, you'll be able to enjoy the important things in your life, including fulfilling your project role. A reasonable life balance will help you stay focused on all of your priorities.

You must also take steps to regain balance if you lose it. One way to do so is to spend time with team members at non-business-related events. Socializing away from the office gives everyone the chance to be themselves, unconfined by corporate convention and project stress. I remember going on impromptu shopping excursions during intense times of a systems integration project in New Jersey. Ten or so of us would blitz the local Marshalls department store and then share our retail bargains over dinner. Having fun and getting to know colleagues better was all it took to regain perspective. It's all about balance.

CHAPTER 28

When Is the Organization Ready for Big Change?

If I had eight hours to chop down a tree, I'd spend
six sharpening my axe.
—Abraham Lincoln

YOU NEED TO BE CONFIDENT that all parts of your organization are ready to take on new ways of working. If people aren't fully prepared they will revert back to old ways of doing things, which in turn will probably lead to business disruptions—orders not being sent, inaccurate inventory records, payments being incorrectly addressed, and so on—mistakes that will cause confusion, frustration, additional cost, and delays. Your goal is to make sure that colleagues are able to say, "I understand why we are making the changes, know what to do, am equipped, and am committed to its success."

Thumbs Down, Thumbs Up

Dr Pepper/Seven Up was the first division of Cadbury to adopt a new computer operating system. The project had been delayed once, but the company was now ramping up for the launch: all project indicators suggested that everything was ready. On a Saturday afternoon, the president visited the office and saw a project programmer working at his desk. He asked, "So, are we ready to go live?" The programmer looked up and said, "Not really." Their conversation led to the president delaying the project for a few months, even after he faced strong opposition from the global implementation team.

The president had lived through a failed systems launch in Australia and knew the pain of not being fully prepared. The distribution system did not work properly, and it was unclear what inventory they had and what had been shipped to customers. This time, his business went live only when such gaps had been closed. He understood that you can't blindly believe in project data, and only when it has been validated should it be acted upon. In this instance, delaying saved the business from a costly failure. He was a hero in a bad situation where organizational readiness procedures did not work. Chance rescues from disaster are not examples of good change management. What would have happened if the president had not shown up?

👍 A regional leader at Cadbury was preparing for a leadership meeting during which the team would decide whether or not to switch over to new computer systems on the planned date. It was a multimillion-dollar decision and, given the cost of mistakes if the company wasn't ready, plus the additional costs of employing a large team for an extended period, he had to get it right. As he prepared for the meeting he asked, "How do I really know if my organization is ready to move to the new systems?" and "What are the questions I need to ask my team so I can assess their readiness?"

The project team helped him create a short list of "killer questions" to assess department readiness. They focused on personal accountability, standards of excellence, and hard evidence of preparedness. He approved the launch date only after each member of his senior team had confirmed readiness. The project was overall a success. The leader understood the importance of gaining personal assurances of readiness to launch.

What Works

Leadership

- Get department leaders to confirm that the necessary preparations have been made. These leaders need to have "skin in the game"—that is, their personal reputations need to be at stake when it comes to the project's success in their business area. This approach also eliminates the "I didn't know" excuse if something goes wrong when the change is made.

- Get leadership teams to sign off on the questions that will be used to assess readiness for the change. Leaders need to be convinced that the questions will provide them with the information they need to make the change. This also engages them in the process and reinforces expectations of readiness.

Process

- Create a colleague validation checklist to confirm readiness for each major phase of the project. Identify what employees need to know at checkpoints, and poll a random sample of individuals across the impacted teams to see how many meet these requirements. Big change happens in three phases—awareness, capability, and sustainability—and each one requires a checkpoint. At the appointed dates, leaders, managers, and project team members should randomly poll colleagues to see if the standards have been met.

Colleague Validation Summary

Date:		One Week Prelaunch:	
Validation points to assess: • Detailed understanding of and ability to execute new business processes and transactions • Detailed understanding of the colleague's role in relation to broader business process • Detailed understanding of transition support and contingency plans			
Checkpoint	**Readiness for Launch**		**Status**
Assessment of leadership team	• Leadership is clear on all checkpoint requirements • Need to answer a few questions on day-one requirements, which will be reviewed again at team meetings prior to launch		Green (ready)
Assessment of line managers	• Most managers are not clear on how to activate contingency plans, which will be covered in department review meetings one week prior to launch		Yellow (plans in place to be ready)
Assessment of colleagues	• Colleagues have demonstrated all checkpoint requirements		Green

*http://www.changewithconfidence.com/?page_id=188

- Ask leaders the following "killer questions":

  - What have you personally done to prepare your team?

  - What evidence do you have that your team is ready to transition (new roles, knowledge, skills, behaviors, relationships, and processes) on the appointed date?

  - How have you prepared your team to be aware of risks, and to know what to do if things go wrong, and how to trigger contingency plans if required?

  - How confident are you that your team is ready to successfully transition? Why do you feel this way?

- Ask colleagues the following "killer questions":

  - What should we be worried about?

  - Are issues getting the right level of attention?

  - How confident are you that you will be able to perform your job on the appointed date?

- Get people active in preparing for the change—job aids, step-by-step procedures, and so on. People are more willing to take on new ways of working if they craft the details and tools themselves.

- Ensure you have a detailed and tested process to resolve issues. Clearly identify who is accountable for raising issues, how they should do so, and how the issues will be reviewed and solved.

- Create a transition checklist for the leadership and project teams to validate:

  - Willingness: Do people feel good about the transition? If not, why not?

  - Leadership: Are leaders aligned and confident?

  - Resources/Budget: Are there enough resources on the ground to support colleagues?

  - Processes: Can colleagues describe how they will work and what will be different from the past? How will they connect with other teams? How will they handle situations that require extra processing (e.g., one-off orders that require manual processing)?

    – Confidence: Do colleagues feel prepared and confident to take on the new ways of working?

- Distribute "what to do" handouts that people can follow on their first few days after the change has been implemented. Include who to contact in large type.

Data/Evidence

- At the start of the project, define the concrete evidence that will confirm colleagues have the knowledge, skills, and behaviors necessary to operate the new ways of working.

- Meet with the trainers to see if there were questions raised during the sessions that haven't been resolved. Typically, a few groups will need extra support in understanding procedures, managing one-off exceptions, and navigating the new processes.

How you prepare colleagues to take on new ways of working must be a core element of your project plan. Also, you will increase your confidence by testing readiness in many ways—leader and colleague interviews, feedback from project team members, and so on. The more positive indicators you get, the more likely transitions will go smoothly.

Resources

CHAPTER 29

How Should We Celebrate Wins?

What every genuine philosopher (every genuine man, in fact) craves most is praise.

—William James

PROJECTS CAN BE GRUELING for you and your team members—uphill battles characterized by tight deadlines, difficult challenges, stretched capabilities, and long hours. In these pressurized environments it is vital that people are rewarded for progress made. Celebrating wins provides breaks from the day-to-day grind, gives you opportunities to recognize work well done, and reinforces the benefits of the change project. Most people want to contribute and be a member of a winning team, and I have found peer recognition to be the ultimate reward for team members. Public acknowledgment that an individual's work is valuable provides personal benefits both at work and at home. (Often, what people tell their loved ones is what they value most.)

Tangible rewards play a significant role, too. Tokens of appreciation, such as a free lunch, a small gift, or movie tickets for team members' families communicate that the team's hard work has not gone unnoticed and is appreciated. It's also the thought behind the effort that counts, and care in selecting rewards will be recognized. Failing to acknowledge good efforts can lead to resentment, apathy, reduced effort, and even poor health. The longer efforts go unnoticed, the more extreme are the negative consequences.

Thumbs Down, Thumbs Up

Zack's Famous Frozen Yogurt is a fast-food franchise based in Louisiana, Missouri. It was booming in the late 1980s and had expanded to Canada. Frozen yogurt was the latest snack trend, and new franchises were being sold weekly. One day, the CEO called the head office team together and said, "I would like to recognize the hard work of three people." He proceeded to talk about what each person had accomplished and ended the ceremony by handing each one a check for $250. My first reaction was "Where's my check?" My partner and I were working around the clock, seven days a week, opening stores across Canada, and this seemed worthy (at the very least) of a similar award. I was happy that my team members were recognized, but why had we been left out? We felt grossly underappreciated. Human reactions like these aren't always rational, but they happen every day. I remember watching other unacknowledged coworkers slowly walking back to their desks after the ceremony, their heads down.

In 2000, Cadbury Chocolate Canada and Trebor Allan merged. The two cultures couldn't have been more different: Cadbury was process-oriented and reserved, Trebor Allan entrepreneurial and (seemingly) eager to pursue any opportunity. The sales teams were run separately for the first year, and both groups held sales conferences in the autumn to plan for the following year. Both meetings had similar content (business updates, training, new product launches, overviews of the following year's goals, etc.) but distinctly different tones. The bulk of Cadbury's meeting budget was allocated toward the venue and production of materials, whereas Trebor Allan spent lavishly on rewarding the sales team through entertainment and gifts. When the sales leader from Trebor Allan was asked why he focused on his colleagues, he said, "Sales people like to be acknowledged. I take care of my people." He understood that people give their best when they are thanked and rewarded. The thought behind his efforts was remembered long after the Cadbury meeting was over and the glossy materials shelved.

What Works

Content

- Don't underestimate the power of small gifts of appreciation—movie passes, gift cards, funny trinkets, plaques, and so on. They matter to people and represent visible badges of success to the rest of the organization.
- Vary the types of recognition you give to maintain excitement.
- Display posters of key milestones across a timeline. When each milestone is reached, replace the posters with an updated timeline. Visual reminders of progress are important.
- Take lots of pictures to document the project. People are motivated by pictures of themselves with their team members performing their roles or celebrating.
- Capture video of colleagues benefiting from the change project and review them with your team.
- Ask your team what you could do to make the project more successful. Your interest in the team's performance is a reward in itself.

Process

- Divide your project into discrete phases. This allows you to celebrate the completion of each phase and show progression along the project timeline (see chart on the next page).
- Schedule recognition events across your project timeline to ensure they are not forgotten and appropriately timed.
- Celebrate early wins (within three months of kickoff), and request acknowledgments from regional or global leaders.
- Be consistent in giving recognition, and be sure to reward everyone who is working hard and achieving results.

Project Milestone Chart

Projects	Jan	Feb	Mar	Apr	May	Jun	Jul	Aug	Sep	Oct	Nov	Dec
Milestones		◇ Kickoff				◇	◇ Testing	◇ Launch				
Recognition activities		◇ Lunch		◇ Arcade evening		◇ Executive visit	◇ Milestone celebration		◇ Post-launch celebration			

Acknowledging efforts by project team members will encourage colleagues to continue giving their best to the project. When done well, recognition creates momentum and motivation, energizing and fortifying the team as colleagues take on tasks and overcome barriers. This assumes that the team has the resources it needs to be successful. If resources are lacking, then recognition and rewards may not be enough to overcome the shortfall.

CHAPTER 30

How Do I Get More Resources If I Need Them?

We find what we expect to find, and we receive what we ask for.
—**Elbert Hubbard**

If you don't ask, the answer is always "no."
—**Tony Robbins**

IN THE PLANNING PHASE, the number and type of resources required are estimated based on the extent and complexity of the change. Since these decisions occur before the change has been implemented, you'll probably need to update your assumptions and tweak the plan when more information becomes available. You may need to reallocate resources or, for larger adjustments, request additional support. Running a project with insufficient resources will force you to make service trade-offs that will leave certain needs unmet. To avoid incurring additional risks to your project, ask for these resources as soon as the need has been identified. Requests for extra resources will be easier if you create awareness of this possibility with the leadership team. Creating a resource request process based on predefined criteria will increase the probability that you will receive approval, and building these requests into project governance will change the focus of the conversation from "Why didn't you know?" to "What is the business need?"

Thumbs Down, Thumbs Up

In 2009, the City of San Diego, the eighth largest municipality in the United States, fired Axon Solutions, which had been hired to implement a new computer system. Additional resources had been committed to the project, which had gone over budget by $11 million, and it was delayed by 10 months. The city cited many poor project management practices, including ineffective resource allocation, not following the agreed-upon change control process, not honoring the agreed-upon division of responsibilities and workload between Axon and city team members, and poor knowledge of the client's business. The city hired SAP, a computer software vendor, for $15.7 million, and the company committed to deploying the resources necessary to complete the project. With a more thorough initial search, San Diego might have gone with SAP in the first place.

A project resource budget had been created for a systems upgrade at Cadbury Adams USA in 2005. It had been approved, and the project team was created. Within months, new information was provided from a sister business on the number of resources required to successfully manage the transition. The original budget was too optimistic and had significantly underestimated the training required, so a one-time budget change proposal was created and approved. The leadership team was not pleased about the additional costs, but it could not refute the evidence submitted. Managing the project properly is a lot cheaper than correcting a poor implementation plan.

What Works

- Include a protocol that states you will review project resources at the beginning of each phase.
- Create a process for reviewing resources based on assessing opportunities and risks.

- Include a fact-based rationale for each resource request. This should include opportunity realization, risk management, and new scope accommodation.

- Identify other options to consider (e.g., reduced scope). The leadership team may think that you haven't done your homework if you do not include this in the proposal.

- Map out the details of your resource requests so leaders have the information needed to make decisions.

Resource Request Summary

Current People Resources	Additional Resources Required	Rationale	Activity	Cost of People Resources	Timing
6	2	• Four additional teams are now converting to the new software system • There are no available colleagues capable of completing this work	• Needs-analysis and training design • Training delivery • Launch support	$48,000	May

*http://www.changewithconfidence.com/?page_id=196

- Minimize the number of resource requests you make. The more requests you make, the more your original plan and your leadership will come into question.

- Revisit a request that is unsuccessful when negative consequences start to arise. More data may change a decision. Even if it doesn't, it's your job to inform leaders of all risks to the business.

Resource requirements may change as you progress through your project, and teams might require more or less support than you originally planned for. It is important to adjust your resource plan accordingly, and, in extreme situations, ask for additional resources. You need to ensure that sufficient resources and people with the right skills are deployed where they are needed most.

CHAPTER 31

How Do I Avoid Losing Team Members?

Autonomy, complexity, and a connection between effort and reward . . . [are] the three qualities that work has to have if it is to be satisfying.
—**Malcolm Gladwell**

AS YOUR PROJECT PROGRESSES, team members will become more and more integrated. They will have accumulated knowledge on the intricacies of the change, developed relationships with fellow team members, and gained a rapport with other colleague groups also in transition. Losing a team member partway through your project means losing knowledge and skills, never mind the "lost" time that it takes to get a new team member up to speed and integrated—and there's always the chance that the new person will not perform well. To safeguard against losing team members you must ensure that your project remains a high priority and that your team members benefit from the experience and therefore resist being moved from the project.

Thumbs Down, Thumbs Up

In 2000, the U.S. Federal Bureau of Investigation hired Science Applications International Corporation (SAIC) to design a new case management software program, the Virtual Case File (VCF), to automate the existing antiquated paper-based system. The new software would

improve the updating of case files, information searches, and the sharing of data among FBI offices. The project was plagued with stakeholder
and project team member changes that led to many system redesigns
and confusion around governance. In October 2001, a newly appointed
FBI director added an experienced special agent to the project team and
created a new senior role, executive assistant director of administration
(EADA), to oversee the project. In turn, she hired an external candidate
to manage all IT projects. She also hired an external candidate to run the
day-to-day operations. (The VCF project had been running for over a year
without a manager.) In November 2002, the SAIC leader left the business and was replaced by another consultant. In April 2003, the EADA
was promoted to another role, as was the special agent consulting on the
project; the new SAIC leader left the project; and the PMO (project
management office) leader resigned, saying that she believed a new FBI
chief information officer (CIO) was going to take control of the project.
"When it's not fun anymore I am not a happy girl,"[1] she said.

In May 2005, the project was canceled. It had cost $200 million, which
was 90 percent over budget. The SAIC's chief operating officer said, "In the
time that SAIC has been working on the project [five years], the FBI has
had 4 different CIOs and 14 different managers. Establishing and setting
system requirements in this environment has been incredibly challenging."[2]

👍 The Water Cube was a showpiece of the 2008 Beijing Olympics, and
hosted the swimming, diving, and water polo events. The vision for the
construction project spoke to the importance of the building to the Beijing
Olympics, and the many firsts it would accomplish. For example, the challenge of implementing innovative design techniques and materials within
an unfamiliar Chinese legal, technological, and social context was seen as
groundbreaking. There were many risks, including developing new tech-
nologies to create the design, managing a complex multinational team
structure, establishing relationships within the Chinese culture, and a tight
timeline (the Chinese government mandated a completion date six months
prior to the Olympics).

One of the biggest concerns was the loss of project team members due to burnout. To mitigate this risk, the project manager organized team members into 20 semi-independent teams so that they could avoid production bottlenecks and unmanageable workloads. Also, they hired specialist project supervisors with technical engineering backgrounds to provide hands-on support when teams were stretched. Furthermore, the quality and frequency of communications were monitored across the teams (located in four countries) to ensure delivery of fast and accurate updates and to avoid delays. The Water Cube was completed on time and on budget, and the public's overwhelming response to the building confirmed that it was unique, a showpiece of Chinese ingenuity for the world to see. The Water Cube's project management was lauded long after the Olympics were over.

What Works

Content

- Make your project the most important initiative in the company: this is your best defense against losing key people.

- Avoid taking percentages of people's time, for example—25 percent of Matt's time. It is difficult taking direction from two (or multiple) bosses. If you must, however, then don't accept less than 50 percent of a person's time. The less time a person devotes to your project, the more likely it is that he or she will be moved from your project, being seen as non-essential to its success.

- Create a team development plan, including self-selected learning objectives for each member. Colleagues are more inclined to want to remain on a team if they feel essential to its success.

- Be clear and definitive when someone asks if one of your team members can be taken off your project. Say no but with a reason—for example, "We are moving into implementation and we need Ken to successfully do so."

Team Development Plan

Team Member	Development Theme	Action	Outcome	Timing
Mel	Analytical rigor	• Develop weekly project status updates • Meet with project manager to discuss potential issues • Present analysis at weekly team meetings	• Created updates • Met project manager biweekly due to scheduling challenges and received feedback on data sourcing and analysis • Presented reviewed analyses monthly	July
Tim	Presentation skills	• Develop monthly project summary presentations • Meet with internal graphic designer to receive feedback on presentations • Present a monthly update at project team meetings	• Developed monthly summaries • Received feedback from Ted and incorporated suggestions into subsequent presentations • Presented update in July	August

*http://www.changewithconfidence.com/?page_id=200

Process

- Get agreement from the executive sponsor at the beginning of the project that losing team members risks success.

- Share the development plans with each team member's manager and HR business partner. This will formalize learning and reinforce its significance.

- Provide opportunities for key members to profile their work to stakeholders. This will help establish their roles and demonstrate the value they bring to the project.

- Formalize the secondment of team members in writing.

- Avoid casually loaning team members to other projects. This will imply that you don't need them.

An intact team is like a well-oiled machine, with all parts performing their roles in unison. Teams are disrupted and can lose momentum when members leave. Shared learnings are no longer understood by everyone, and assumptions can lead to frustration and mistakes being made. Even though some staffing changes are unavoidable, putting effort into maintaining your team is your best defense against losing key people.

CHAPTER 32

What Do I Do If Someone Is Pulled from My Team?

We trained hard, but it seemed every time we were beginning
to form up into teams, we would be reorganized.
—Charlton Ogburn

DESPITE YOUR BEST EFFORTS, business priorities or personal circumstances can change your team roster. Many leaders believe that losing a team member will have little impact on team dynamics. This is rarely true. Teams develop connections, rapport, and alignment based on shared experiences, and a new team member can disrupt this positive and evolving dynamic. They will need to be brought up to speed, which causes lower productivity as they learn and others train them. Unless the exiting colleague is a poor performer, your productivity will be reduced when team changes are made. Things won't work the way they used to, some tasks will take longer to complete, mistakes will be made, and, if not managed well, people will become demoralized.

Thumbs Down, Thumbs Up

In 2006, Cadbury Adams Canada set up a cross-departmental team to create a five-year business strategy. Two key team members were promoted to new roles in the middle of the project. They still attended meetings but didn't have the capacity to facilitate or drive the project. Work continued but lost momentum because these changes weren't immediately addressed. As a cofacilitator, I didn't manage the gap. The process would have been far more effective if the team had regrouped to discuss changing roles and requirements. I did not fully appreciate that a change in personnel changes roles, accountabilities, and expectations for others. Without discussing the changes, assumptions were made about who would take on additional responsibilities, and this led to confusion and disappointment when nothing changed.

👍 The first major London 2012 Olympics construction project was the removal and underground relocation of overhead power lines at the Olympic Park site. So as not to delay other projects, the job needed to be completed in half the time industry standards suggested would be necessary. Planning for the Powerlines Undergrounding project began in 2005 by the London Development Agency *before* the 2012 Olympics host was selected. When England's proposal won, the project was transferred to the Olympic Delivery Authority, a new agency responsible for building all new venues and infrastructure. The project team planned for this transition from the outset, and its planning proved helpful when a new project manager came on board five months into the project. Governance and communication channels had been well documented—speeding up orientation—and the project and contractor teams were colocated, facilitating quick introductions. Also, meetings on issues like risk mitigation were held daily, making it easier to learn about latest developments. The £259 million project was completed on time and on budget in 2008 and was used as a benchmark and source of motivation for all other London 2012 projects.

What Works

- Fill resource gaps as quickly as possible. They place extra work on the rest of the team.

- Negotiate ample time to transition knowledge and experience—including technical and social information—from exiting to new team members.

- Engage leaving team members in the selection of their successors. They will know what capabilities and personal styles are required.

- Write a formal orientation plan for new team members (see chart on the next page). Phasing in the activities over the first month will minimize strains on resources and help avoid information overload.

- Hold a meeting on the new team member's first day and ask each recruit to introduce him- or herself and his or her role. Then, share successes and challenges to date.

- Host good-bye events for leaving team members—a lunch, an afternoon get-together, or drinks outside the office.

- Ask leaving team members for feedback on the project and your leadership style. They may provide perspectives that you were not aware of.

- Publicly thank the exiting team members for their contributions. Failing to do so, or worse, discrediting colleagues because they choose to leave your team will lessen the trust that other team members have in you as a leader.

Casey Stengel once said, "Getting good players is easy. Getting 'em to play together is the hard part." This holds true for teams that acquire new team members. Usually, there is a sense of loss for the team member that has left and a period of uncertainty as his or her replacement becomes integrated. You must engineer a smooth transition by providing a thorough orientation program.

New Team Member Orientation Plan

Activity	Attendees	Purpose	Timing (by end of)			
			Week 1	Week 2	Week 3	Week 4
Welcome meeting	All team members	• Share project developments to date • Understand issues and opportunities • Review current initiatives	X			
Briefing meetings	Each team member	• Provide overview of his or her role • Share perspectives of the new team member's role—e.g., work to be done, success factors, challenges, etc. • Answer questions and provide clarifications	X	X		
Introduction meetings for stakeholders	Each stakeholder associated with the role	• Gain an understanding of stakeholder needs • Understand issues and opportunities • Review current phase of project			X	X

*http://www.changewithconfidence.com/?page_id=204

CHAPTER 33

How Do I Keep the Project Team Energized?

The deepest urge in human nature is the desire to be important.
—John Dewey

CHANGE PROJECTS CAN BE EXHAUSTING. Managing tight timelines, increased workloads, and navigating through challenges can drain team members. It is important to keep them motivated and energized so they maintain a whatever-it-takes attitude while avoiding burnout.

Big change projects tend to exact more emotional strain than nonproject roles. There is constant pressure to drive forward on a difficult course that is heavily monitored. Many tasks, if delayed, cause other teams to fall behind, creating a steam-cooker environment where each mistake or missed deadline can threaten the entire project. In such pressurized environments it is essential to balance the negative effects of stress with positive recognition, opportunities to recharge, and rewards. Acknowledging people's efforts and pacing their work will give them the energy needed to succeed over the long haul.

Thumbs Down, Thumbs Up

Dr Pepper/Seven Up underwent a complex SAP implementation project that encountered numerous delays, and the company was forced to extend an 18-month timeline to 36 months. After each delay, plans were recast and team members had to adjust their activities. After 24 months, some team members felt they had been away from the regular business for too long and requested their old jobs back. As there was no reentry plan for these employees, some team members left the business for external opportunities. The company lost good talent because it failed to keep the project team motivated and convince the members that their interests were being looked after. Colleagues will give the benefit of doubt to an organization for a while, but rarely forever.

👍 Volunteers from the Canadian Cadbury Adams systems integration project formed a social committee and were given a small budget for group activities. They planned a different event every month at venues selected to profile Toronto, where the project was based, as many team members were commuters from the United States. Each activity was well received and a topic of conversation for the rest of the week. People looked forward to the events and felt closer to their teammates after attending them. (Some of the more distinctive ones, like a ghost tour of downtown Toronto and whirlyball—like lacrosse played in bumper cars—were talked about many years after the project was completed.) Providing time for team members to unwind and get to know each other is essential. Informal relationships promote familiarity, companionship, and trust, the foundation stones for collaboration and collective effort.

What Works

- Be as energetic and optimistic as you want your team to be.

- Brand the initiative. Create an inspirational project name and tagline.

- Create and maintain an environment of success. When faced with problems, show confidence that the team can solve them, and reinforce the idea that teams win together.

- Pace your team so team members don't burnout. The signs are clear when a team is overworked and colleagues are running out of energy.

- Use humor to liven up project working sessions—it will pay big dividends.
- Give out small gifts along the way; their symbolism is important.
- Stand up for the team if it is under pressure or being criticized. A team needs its leader to support it when being challenged.

Process

- Prepare people for their new working environment—tight timelines, long hours, and so on. Surprises are stressful.
- Create a team activity plan to ensure rewards are distributed across the project, and avoid long periods without acknowledgments (see chart on the next page).
- Include time in your team meetings to share wins. This will set a positive mood for your team and provide opportunities for you to acknowledge progress.
- Provide short breaks for your team to recharge its batteries after demanding phases of the project.

Teams, like individuals, have varying levels of energy. A motivated team is focused, uses its strengths, and is effective at managing stress. You can achieve these ends by making the project exciting, pacing the team, and providing your colleagues with time to get to know each other better. This also is true for stakeholders as you help them manage their roles.

Team Activity Plan

WHEN? Target Date	WHAT? Reward	WHO? Audience	WHY? Objective	Comment
September 1	Team event: dinner and mini-golf game	Team members	• Completed the planning phase • Kickoff implementation phase	Executive sponsor will address the group at dinner and acknowledge team achievement
November 15	Team break: ice cream bar	Team and steering committee members	• Motivate team as they prepare for launch • Thank team for efforts	Project manager will serve ice cream from a portable ice cream cart

*http://www.changewithconfidence.com/?page_id=208

Communication

CHAPTER 34

How Do I Manage My Stakeholders?

There is nothing more difficult to plan, more doubtful of success, nor more dangerous to manage than a new system. The initiator has the enmity of all who would profit by the preservation of the old institution and merely lukewarm defenders in those who gain by the new ones.

—Niccolò Machiavelli

STAKEHOLDERS ARE LEADERS who influence the direction (and evaluation) of your change project. The leadership team and steering committee are internal stakeholders. Other leaders who report to them can also be stakeholders depending on their connection to the project. For example, an IT director may not be impacted by new sales software but influences the project because it's his or her team doing the work. Supporting such people is one of your most important roles. It requires helping them fulfill their commitments to the project and ensuring that they get what they need from it. To do this you must keep stakeholders informed and involved at all times. If you don't, your project will be disrupted, be viewed as being poorly run, or simply fail.

An important aspect of good stakeholder management is to know them well. Each one will have his or her own objectives, beliefs, and interests tied to your project. Does the project help or hurt their agendas? Are there any "must haves" that they will fight for? How do they like to be informed? What are their hot buttons? The more you know about your stakeholders, the better able you will be to support and manage them.

The political environment of your organization *will* impact your project, and some leaders might not support an initiative that another is sponsoring. Complicating the picture is a leader benefiting from the status quo who stands to lose a lot by the new change. It is your job to navigate stakeholder dynamics so your change project is not negatively affected by personal agendas.

Thumbs Down, Thumbs Up

In 2007, the German Federal Ministry of Youth commissioned the design of a social networking website called Du-machst.de, through which young people could interact about civic projects. Members could set up profiles, add "friends," send messages, and create civic project proposals that could be submitted for government funding.

The project ran into trouble when a stakeholder who hadn't been briefed on the timeline announced a launch date months ahead of the website being built and tested. The project team also failed to allay stakeholder fears about Internet security and the negative press likely coming from posting unedited member comments online. The project team had access to success stories from other government agencies that had launched similar websites but did not take the time to share them. The website attracted only 200 registered members—who posted just three messages—and was closed the following year.

The project manager of the Cadbury Adams North American operating systems integration was superb at stakeholder management and, in 2005, he structured his role so that most of his time was spent with these key people. A master of the social game, he understood their needs, gave them updates, and constantly cajoled them. Beyond interacting with them at formal steering committee meetings, he continually checked in with leaders to ask them about their concerns, and he always looked ahead, sharing proposals with senior influencers before decision-making meetings to make sure they were on side. One of his mantras was "I don't want surprises," and he rarely saw them. His understanding of stakeholder needs and his excellent communication skills led to their acceptance and support. At the end of the project he was acknowledged for his excellent management skills and promoted shortly thereafter.

What Works

Process

- Create a stakeholder analysis chart and a dashboard to efficiently communicate information (see charts on the next two pages). This will facilitate a logical flow to your updates and will clearly demonstrate progress made on your project.

- Review and update your initial Stakeholder Analysis based on ongoing meetings with stakeholders.

- Do your best to include the CEO (or most senior leader) as a stakeholder, and coach him or her appropriately. CEOs may not see your project as requiring their direct attention, but if you can convince them of this need, your project will get more resources and exposure.

- Set up regular meetings with each stakeholder, ideally weekly, and ask what type of information the stakeholder would find valuable and the format he or she would like to receive it in. Include information you believe important (e.g., next steps, briefings on decisions that need to be made, accomplishments, etc.).

- Review your Stakeholder Analysis before every stakeholder meeting. This will help you prepare for the meeting and enable you to regularly update information.

- Always have next steps for each stakeholder so your project stays top-of-mind. Actions like leading update sessions, demonstrating new behaviors, and collecting feedback on team readiness are essential to the success of your project.

Stakeholder Analysis Update

Stakeholders in New Innovation Process	How Will They Benefit?	How Will They Lose?	What Support Do I Need/Has Been Offered?	How Motivated Are They about the Project?	What Actions Do I Need to Take to Maximize Benefits?	By When?
Marketing director	• Less rework; more new product projects • Greater department participation	• Speed of decision making is slightly slower—cross-departmental	• Sponsor process changes • Communications to organization	Very	• Develop strong design guiding principles • Drive project with speed	January January–June
Sales director	• Earlier input into product decisions	• **Update: final veto of new product design resides with global director**	• Communications to Sales team	Neutral	• Reinforce customer benefits of greater product launch execution versus current service gap • **Update: Build awareness of customer involvement in new product development**	January March
Supply Chain director	• Greater visibility of new product development		• Communications to Supply Chain	Supportive	• Reinforce production efficiencies	January

Stakeholder Dashboard Update

Current Status	Upcoming

Follow-Up Items from Last Meeting	**Key Upcoming Activities and Decisions**
– Replacement of Sales team member – Cost-savings task force questions – Confirmation of holiday blackout period dates	– Gain input from engagement sessions – Review prototype with cross-function representatives – Review prototype with leadership team

Accomplishments & Status	**Key Milestones**	**Date**
	– Design prototype process	February 15
– Scheduled all engagement sessions – Started biweekly project team meetings – Agreed on design methodology	– Prototype review with cross-function representatives	March 7
	– Prototype review with leadership team	March 20

Issues/Open Items
– Governance process for "go"/"no go" decisions – Lack of best practice examples

*http://www.changewithconfidence.com/?page_id=215

Relationships

- Identify how your project (and you personally) can contribute to a stakeholder's overall agenda. This might be a key differentiator between you and other project managers.

- Build realistic expectations of what success looks like. (Stakeholders might have unrealistic expectations because they don't see the complexity of the changes or the risks involved with implementation.)

- Get stakeholders to come to you first when they have an issue. This will avoid concerns being circulated before the project team can address them.

Stakeholders can be your biggest supporters or your biggest detractors. Working to keep them informed and managing their expectations will build strong relationships that will help make your project a success. As with all relationships, demonstrating your interest in the needs of others encourages them to reciprocate.

CHAPTER 35

How Can I Minimize Change Fatigue?

Many people feel they must multi-task because everybody else is multi-tasking, but this is partly because they are all interrupting each other so much.

—Marilyn vos Savant

MOST LARGE ORGANIZATIONS have numerous change projects running at the same time. Organizational, departmental, and work group projects coexist with daily operating activities, and if you don't plan your project with this in mind, you will add stress to the company and jeopardize getting the full support of those assigned to your project.

The negative effects of continual, multiple initiatives running at one time are many. The business environment is mired with unclear priorities, constant distractions, intense time pressure, lack of control, and role and career ambiguity. If left unchecked, colleagues will experience change fatigue, and lose the energy and wherewithal to fully contribute. This leads to fear, frustration, and diminishing performance.

Many businesses don't have formal mechanisms to limit, prioritize, and, if necessary, cancel low-performing projects. Some cultures operate with a "more is better" mind-set and create more work than can be physically delivered. A "we just have to get everything done" operating philosophy generally leads to poor execution and colleague burnout. In this type of environment, colleagues juggle their responsibilities daily, deciding which requests to honor and which to ignore. This is a dangerous backdrop for a change leader who needs focused business support to adopt new ways of working. Proactive management is the best way to secure the full availability of your resources.

Thumbs Down, Thumbs Up

With over 1,000 stores, roughly 140,000 employees, and $3.25 billion in annual sales, Loblaw is Canada's largest food distributor. In 2009, Loblaw commenced a company-wide IT systems overhaul to institute new processes across order management, inventory, pricing, financials, and human resources, as well as for its master data. Other big change projects in play at the same time included a five-year supply chain systems optimization, a retail operations reorganization, a merchandizing efficiency project, a new store time and attendance system, a major "own label" product line launch, and store renovations and openings. Independent change management teams managed these projects using varying methodologies. Other challenges included changes in leadership and project teams, and change requests. The IT system completion date was delayed from 2011 to 2012 and is currently slated for 2013–14.

This massive change agenda (costing up to $2.6 billion in total) may continue to grow given aggressive competitors like Walmart (spending $750 million on its stores in 2012) and Target (slated to enter the Canadian grocery market in 2013), requiring change teams to keep colleagues engaged through a prolonged and likely very painful process. Did the ever-present anxiety about losing market share outweigh the risk of the company imploding because of too much change, or was it the belief that Loblaw was too big to fail? In 2012, when the company reported a 22 percent drop in first-quarter profits, the executive chairman said, "We are confident that our ongoing investment in infrastructure will set the stage for future earnings growth."[1] Ultimately, the success of these changes rests with the employees who must adopt them, and their ability to be productive in their dynamic environment will set the stage for future competitiveness.

👍 In 2006, when Microsoft released Windows Vista to corporations, Microsoft Netherlands piloted "the 'New World of Work' (changing the way people work to maximize their potential), 'Digital Workstyle' (virtual collaborative working), and 'People-Ready' (empowerment to build the work environment that suits their needs) visions of Bill Gates and Microsoft Corporate."[2]

Employees were asked to cocreate more effective ways of working, including the development of better collaboration and communications practices. The process increased awareness of project communications and what Microsoft called organizational fitness: "The capacity to learn and change to fit new circumstances."[3] Increased employee empowerment led to a greater flexibility of work styles, a greater influence on how work was done, increased employee satisfaction, and higher productivity.[4]

What Works

- Create a project timeline that minimizes resource and communications conflicts with other projects (see chart on the next page). Review this with the leadership team to demonstrate good project management within the total business environment.

- Survey business representatives to ensure they can contribute to your project. Address situations where team members are failing to complete their regular role and project tasks.

- Adopt existing templates so that employees do not have to learn different formats.

- Raise resource conflicts with the leadership team so they can be managed within the overall priorities of the business.

- Encourage leaders to consider available resource capacity before approving additional projects.

Project Timeline Summary

Project	Jan	Feb	Mar	Apr	May	Jun	Jul	Aug	Sep	Oct	Nov	Dec
Project 1		◇ Kickoff					◇ Testing	◇ Launch				
Project 2		◇ Kickoff					◇	◇ Testing			◇ Launch	
Project 3			◇ Kickoff					Testing	◇	◇ Launch		

*http://www.changewithconfidence.com/?page_id=221

There is only so much an organization can manage at one time. When businesses take on too much, people "manage by triage," completing urgent (but maybe not important) tasks first. They suffer change fatigue when this dynamic spreads across a team or business and becomes part of the culture. Being mindful of potential conflicts is the first step to resolving them, and marrying your plan with other project plans will help avoid situations where colleagues are forced to manage multiple responsibilities. Also, quickly addressing conflicts will avoid over-committing colleagues and fragmenting their efforts. Quality of effort is more important than quantity, and being overworked is one reason for poor performance. Resistance is another.

CHAPTER 36

How Do I Overcome Resistance?

Any significant transformation creates "people issues."
New leaders will be asked to step up, jobs will be changed,
new skills and capabilities must be developed, and employees
will be uncertain and resistant.

—John Jones

RESISTANCE TO LARGE ORGANIZATIONAL CHANGE is natural. People tend to fear what they don't know or understand, and colleagues will focus on imagined negative consequences when they sense that life as they know it will change. Adopting something new raises the possibility of instability, losing something of value, more work, and personal failure, and if these perceptions are not managed, people will resist change.

Identifying the reasons for resistance—everything from passive compliance, indifference, or apathy, to outright sabotage—and addressing them up front will neutralize these roadblocks. Also, doing so can help identify gaps in your plan for colleague transition. You will be in a better position to implement the plan if you're aware of concerns and proactively manage them.

Thumbs Down, Thumbs Up

Canada Post, a $7.3-billion Crown corporation, announced a five-year modernization program in 2007 to become more profitable, efficient, and competitive. Specifically, the goals were to become a leader in home delivery for Internet purchases, build its digital presence, and aggressively defend its regular delivery systems. Revenues were threatened by declining traditional mail volumes (a drop of 17 percent from 2005 to 2012) and the growing popularity of electronic alternatives and private carriers. Also, the corporation's costs were increasing because of its mandate to offer services to all Canadian addresses regardless of profitability, the use of aging processing equipment, and suboptimal operating processes.

Labor relations were strained throughout the modernization process and intensified in 2011 when a new collective agreement could not be reached, prompting revolving strikes and a management lockout of 48,000 unionized employees (which cost $220 million). The government intervened and ordered employees to accept a contract worse than the one they had rejected (because of Canada Post's financial situation), further lowering morale.

Management was not successful in convincing employees that less generous pension plans, more flexible salary structures, and greater flexibility in scheduling were necessary for the corporation to survive. (The business plan for the transformation had not been made public, and employees had little input into modernization projects.) A Canada Post customer commented, "The carriers themselves would be a wonderful source of possible work improvements if only they could get their managers to listen."[1] Employees resisted changes implemented to streamline the postal delivery model. Letter carriers' roles changed from sorting and delivering mail to being responsible for all duties within their territory—sorting; driving a mail truck; delivering letters, flyers, and parcels; and collecting outgoing mail from mail boxes, small businesses, and Canada Post retail stores. Letter carriers were also required to operate personal data terminals that scanned packages and tracked locations. One employee said, "I've heard that our president and CEO is not of the flesh; he's a supercomputer floating on a cooling barge in the Atlantic Ocean."[2] Another added, "Stress levels are up and the mail isn't being delivered—either on time, or at all . . . I take pride in what I do, as do most of my colleagues, but we can't do our jobs under these new conditions."[3] Canada Post recorded a $253-million loss in 2011, its first in 16 years.

👍 In 2005, Cadbury Trebor Allan was forced to downsize and become more competitive in an aggressive market. It was a four-horse battle for chocolate sales, with Nestlé, Hershey's, and Mars all vying for increased market share, even though sales across the board were growing at less than 5 percent annually. Increased sales for one company meant taking them away from another, and all four companies were prepared to invest to grow.

This was the first downsizing the company had gone through, and everyone needed help to manage it. At an all-managers meeting, the leadership team briefed the managers on the need for the initiative, how decisions would be made, and the important role they would play. The team was given training and an overview of the tools it would have to support its groups. Considerable time was allotted for managers to ask questions about the change and their personal futures.

The day before the downsizing announcement, the managers were brought together again to review the communications materials, and a debrief session was scheduled for the following day. Although some managers were personally impacted by the changes, the feedback was positive on how the project was managed. Respect, fairness, participation, and support are especially important when managing a project with negative consequences for colleagues. "I wish I didn't have to leave this wonderful company," said one female colleague.

What Works

- Identify potential sources of resistance before you implement the project plan (see chart on page 176). Find out what current ways of working employees don't want to give up. The team kickoff meeting is a good place to start this research.

- Discuss potential reasons for resistance with colleagues when you describe the project vision to the organization, and reinforce the positive benefits of the change.

- Build in as much certainty as you can—what is going to happen and when, what aspects will change and what will stay the same, and so on. Reduce stress and fear by reducing the unknown.

- Demonstrate how your team will prepare colleagues to take on new ways of working and make sure that managers have all the tools they need to support the change.

- Identify "early adopters" who support the change. Ensure they have the necessary information and are invited to forums where they can influence other colleagues.

- Avoid publicly challenging people who show resistance. The larger population may look on these people as underdogs and become sympathetic, especially if they have social clout in the organization. Also, this will encourage resistance to go underground, making it difficult to identify and manage.

Resistance generally results from negative perceptions of the change underway. This is something that needs to be understood before it can be managed and then removed. As John F. Kennedy said, "Peace is a daily, a weekly, a monthly process, gradually changing opinions, slowly eroding old barriers, quietly building new structures." Once you know the source of resistance, you can take action to relieve concerns and build support for new ways of working. Only through patient dialogue will you be able to change resisters into enablers, but sometimes the biggest resisters become your biggest allies.

Resistance Analysis

Area	Source of Resistance	Evidence	Action	Outcome	Next Step
Human Resources	Concern over leading training sessions	• Some HR colleagues have expressed concerns about leading training sessions • A few have refused to participate in train-the-trainer activities	• Identify members willing to be trainers • Adopt a "lead and support" approach where an experienced facilitator is paired with someone less experienced (and the experienced facilitator delivers most of the program) • Provide a train-the-trainer skills program before the selection of training pairs • Monitor initial sessions and adjust roles based on feedback	• Assessment of trainer skills • Increased training capability • Qualified trainer teams pairs selected • Reduced stress of trainers	• Conduct train-the-trainer session • Assess training capabilities • Review pilot sessions with broader HR team

*http://www.changewithconfidence.com/?page_id=225

CHAPTER 37

How Do I Know Communications Are Working?

The single biggest problem in communication is the illusion that it has taken place.

—George Bernard Shaw

The less people know, the more they yell.

—Seth Godin

IF COMMUNICATION IS DONE PROPERLY, colleagues are clear about the need for change, what is required to make the project successful, and how it is progressing. If it is done poorly, they are unclear about how the organization (and they themselves) will benefit from the project, what is needed from them for the project to be successful, and how it is doing. I have never seen a project succeed without strong communications.

Developing a communications plan is a necessary first step in becoming an effective communicator. It should map out the how, what, where, and when aspects of informing colleagues about the project. This doesn't guarantee that you will communicate effectively: an equally important step is to monitor the quality of delivery to ensure that objectives are met. If they are not met, changes must be made to the plan. If you don't monitor communication effectiveness, you could be fooled into thinking your plan is working when it's not. A gap here between vision and reality will disenfranchise the very people you need to make your change successful.

You must create feedback mechanisms to test the effectiveness of your communications plan. Beyond verifying whether colleagues know and understand your key messages, you need feedback on whether people perceive the communications as transparent, open, and honest. When colleagues have a high level of trust, they usually have a high level of engagement.

Thumbs Down, Thumbs Up

In 2009, Cadbury decided to change its business structure to become a more integrated and efficient company. It adopted a matrix organization structure based on dual-reporting relationships wherein leaders had a function department head and a national division boss. For example, a head of marketing in Japan would move from having one boss, his or her Japan country president, to two, adding the global head of marketing. This change was a dramatic departure from Cadbury's traditional linear management structure.

The global project team put considerable effort into outlining the changes associated with the new model. Nonetheless, at a regional meeting six months after the launch, it was clear that the national division leadership teams were not aware of the extensive changes they were expected to make. The regional leaders had assumed that the new structure didn't materially affect the national divisions and chose not to pass the detailed information on to them. The country leadership teams felt misinformed and became resistant to the changes. By not following up to ensure communications had been received the way they were intended, a project team risks that incorrect messages will take root and colleagues will respond negatively.

Kraft Foods distributed a quarterly survey where a random sample of employees were asked for feedback on company communications. It provided a "pulse check" on how a 100,000-plus-employee global organization rated the effectiveness of internal communications. During the Kraft Cadbury merger, questions were added to measure people's awareness of the details of the integration. Respondents were divided into two groups—colleagues from the acquiring company and from the one being acquired—and the data confirmed that employees from both groups were nervous about the merger. It also dispelled rumors that only employees from the acquired company had such feelings, a realization that helped script future integration messages. Seeking employee feedback on how they perceive communications is the best way of validating their effectiveness. Incorporating the feedback in future communications is the best way to improve it.

What Works

- Treat colleagues undergoing change as internal clients. This mind-set will help you set the tone of your communications.

- Review final drafts of communications with a few colleagues from each area of your organization. This will ensure that the messages are received as intended.

- Ask leadership team members to poll their teams. This will provide a good cross-section of data and engage senior stakeholders in your project.

- Use employee surveys and focus groups to get feedback on communications (see chart on the next page), current levels of awareness, and unaddressed information needs.

- Record verbatim comments from focus groups, and provide space for them to be put into questionnaires. Often such direct testimony provides the deepest and most insightful feedback on how a project is being perceived.

- Consistently ask the same monitoring questions so you can demonstrate movement over time.

People are the real judges of your communications, and it is vital that you test the effectiveness of your words. Asking employees to share their perceptions of the information they receive will allow you to gauge what has registered correctly and what needs to be recommunicated. As with other aspects of your plan, if something is not being communicated properly, you must correct it.

Employee Survey

Statement	Strongly Disagree	Disagree	Neither Agree nor Disagree	Agree	Strongly Agree
I feel appropriately updated on project Y				X	

Statement			Too Little	Just Right	Too Much
Based on the information you have received so far, the level of detail is			X		
Based on the information you have received so far, the frequency is				X	

Question			Comment		
How could we improve communications?			Communications could be improved by sharing what feedback points are being adopted. I assume that feedback is not being used when I hear nothing about the changes that have been made. It would be helpful to incorporate project Y updates at regional meetings.		

CHAPTER 38

How Do I Get a Leader Back On Side?

Whenever you're in conflict with someone, there is one factor that can make the difference between damaging your relationship and deepening it. That factor is attitude.
—William James

I have always thought the actions of men the best interpreters of their thoughts.
—John Locke

IT'S COMMON FOR AT LEAST ONE LEADER to diverge from a leadership role during your project. Examples of this include exhibiting old or contrary behaviors, making negative statements, and failing to attend activities such as executive update meetings. Whatever it is, the lapse must be addressed quickly because it will be perceived as permission for others to do the same, which can lead to mob mentality, a phenomenon virtually impossible to reverse.

Divergent behavior is symptomatic of opposition or indifference to your project. Leaders will diverge because they are not pleased with an aspect of the project, or because they forget what behaviors they should be demonstrating, probably because they don't care. The longer you delay approaching such a leader, the more likely the divergent behavior will appear acceptable and the harder it will be to eliminate.

Thumbs Down, Thumbs Up

👎 In 1994, while I was working for the Business Development Bank of Canada, a client launched a company-wide customer service training program. The leader kicked it off by thanking his team for attending the first meeting and acknowledged the importance of the program for the business's future. Then, when asked if he was going to attend the full session, incredibly, said he didn't have time for "these things."

Once the session started, the facilitator visited the leader and persuaded him to attend the action-planning presentations, pointing out that if the leader didn't have time for the initiative his team wouldn't either. The leader agreed to attend and reiterated the importance of the project. What he didn't initially realize was that his actions spoke louder than his words; if he didn't "walk the talk," his team wouldn't either. By attending only the action-planning session, he demonstrated that the program was worthy of his time, but only some of it. This tepid response was picked up by the team members, who reacted in kind—tepidly. The leader didn't follow up on progress made on the action plans, and the initiative failed, confirming the participants' initial suspicions.

👍 Toronto-Dominion (TD) Bank, one of the top 10 financial services companies on the continent, was named the "best bank in North America" for three straight years—between 2009 and 2011—by *Euromoney* magazine. In 2010, TD Bank implemented a new risk mitigation system. When the executive sponsor saw the prototype of it, he told the project team that he was paying a lot of money for something that looked like Excel and should look (and feel) like Amazon.com. His comments telegraphed that he hadn't been part of the design and didn't see value in the solution proposed. The project team created a briefing document outlining how the new system would solve existing business issues, and included testimonials from business users. They also redesigned the project website to operate and look like Amazon.com. Once the executive sponsor saw its benefits and the improved website, he gave the project his full support, touting it to his peers and demonstrating it to the board of directors.

What Works

- When approaching a leader who is off track:

  - Confirm that the misaligned behavior did occur; that is, put the actual facts on the table.

  - Ask them why this happened.

  - Communicate the impact of the leader's actions, which he or she may not be aware of.

  - Wait for his or her response (if the behavior was an oversight, the leader will often acknowledge the gap and agree to get back on board).

  - Ask what he or she thinks will remedy the issue.

  - Agree to next steps before leaving the meeting.

- If a leader refuses to adjust his or her behavior, suggest that you both meet with the executive sponsor to discuss the matter. Do this only in the worst-case scenario, as the leader may hold a grudge against you and the project for escalating the issue.

- Ask for permission to point out any additional gaps in the future, even though your role is to do so. Leaders appreciate this gesture of respect.

Colleagues model their behavior based on how leaders act. You must intervene immediately when leaders' conduct is at odds with the future state you are trying to create. Sometimes leaders will correct their actions once you point out the problem and other times they won't. Either way, speed is key to minimizing damage done by leaders' divergent behavior.

CHAPTER 39

How Do I Get a New Business Leader's Support?

Ask yourself what the owners want.
—Bill Dauphinais and Paul Pederson

LEADERSHIP CHANGES HAPPEN all the time. When a leader gets moved into a new role or leaves the company, you must work with his or her replacement. The problem is that the replacement doesn't know the details of your project or have any particular allegiance to it. It is important to quickly establish a relationship with the new leader and get to know his or her interests and priorities. You can then frame your project within this context, and you'll be more likely to get a positive response.

I have seen many instances where a project continues under a new leader's direction but does not receive the attention it needs for success. The worst-case scenario is when your project is seen as part of the last leader's agenda rather than part of a long-term business strategy. New leaders are repelled by past agendas and successes because they will never be attributed to them regardless of their ongoing efforts. Linking your project to the new leader's agenda is the best way of maintaining its status and level of support.

Thumbs Down, Thumbs Up

In 1954, the government of New South Wales, Australia, decided to build a new opera house in Sydney. Construction of the winning design began in 1959, and most of the exterior was completed by 1965, when a new government was elected. The new premier transferred jurisdiction for the project to the Ministry of Public Works. The architect was unable to gain the support of the new minister for his already approved design and construction plan. The minister of Public Works abruptly refused to approve construction of prototypes for the building's interiors and stopped paying the architect, which meant he could not pay his staff and suppliers. The architect resigned from the project once his resources were depleted, and new local architects were hired. They completely changed the initial designs, requiring millions of dollars in stage equipment to be scrapped. The Sydney Opera House opened in 1973 at a cost of $102 million, 15 times the estimated budget. In 1999, a different government agency rehired the original architect to change the interiors back to the original designs.

👍 The Millennium Dome in London, England, opened to the public on December 31, 1999, just hours before fear of the Y2K computer software meltdown subsided. The "Dome," the largest dome in the world, housed The Millennium Experience, an educational exhibit celebrating the third millennium.

Originally, the Conservative government conceived of the project as smaller in size and scope. In 1997, when the Labour government came to power, Tony Blair, the new prime minister, toured the proposed site, and his new minister responsible for the project inspected a scale model of it with the former chief executive and cultural secretary. The prime minister saw the potential of the project and personally supported it, significantly expanding the scale of the exhibit and its budget despite widespread concern expressed by many cabinet advisors. He said: "We now propose an exhibition which will make a statement for the whole nation at the dawn of the millennium. It will open a window on the future; the future for individuals; for society; the environment and the world."[1] The Dome became a symbol of Tony Blair's leadership and his government that he saw as an achievement of a "new Britain."

What Works

- Schedule a new-leader briefing to orient him or her to your project. Tell the story of the project, and describe why it was initiated (the business case), the benefits it will bring, early wins, and lessons learned to date.

Before a new leader can support a project, he or she must understand what it is, what it is trying to accomplish, and where it's at.

Kickoff Meeting Agenda

Agenda
Objectives
Executive sponsor/project manager opening (thank-you)
Outcomes/deliverables (including measurements and dashboard)
High-level overview of plan
Project results to date
Lessons learned—What worked and what could have been better?
Leader's role
Next milestones and deliverables (and leader support required)

*http://www.changewithconfidence.com/?page_id=235

- Invite leaders and stakeholders to give their impressions of the project. Such testimonials will create powerful commendations for the entire group.

- Encourage the new leader to provide input and suggest changes. You will have a greater chance of gaining support for your project if the new leader can put his or her mark on it.

- Review the leader's role and check that the project is something he or she will endorse. If you hit a brick wall, discuss what other leader could take over the role.

New leaders present a risk to your project. You must quickly meet with them to understand their agendas and demonstrate how your project will contribute to them. Appealing to leaders' egoes or vanity may be necessary—leaders are human, too, and need personal validation, especially since they are likely insecure about taking on their new roles. The best way to ensure support is to give them ownership of the project by helping them put their personal stamps on it. A successful change manager knows how to quietly influence human emotions, all the while managing his or her own anxieties.

CHAPTER 40

What Do I Do When I Don't Know What to Do?

The true test of character is not how much we know how
to do, but how we behave when we don't know what to do.
—John W. Holt Jr.

DURING BIG CHANGE PROJECTS, leaders typically face issues they have never experienced before. The cross-departmental nature of these assignments adds complexities that are different from issues within departments: organization-wide solutions that meet multiple stakeholders' needs are required. How you manage these challenges is important because this will define your leadership style and perceived capability. Your stakeholders and team members will be watching how you react in pressurized situations and will form their conclusions accordingly. You need to take charge, keep focused, and marshal resources toward solving problems and creating the needed change. You may need to fake optimism when there are no signs of resolution, otherwise people may become paralyzed and worsen the situation. If you are not confident, no one else will be.

Your career is on the line when managing big change projects, and you will be positively regarded as someone with future potential if you demonstrate grace under pressure. On the other hand, your reputation will be negatively affected if you panic or are seen to lack confidence. How you manage difficult situations will be remembered long after people forget what you actually did.

Thumbs Down, Thumbs Up

👎 In 2005, the Cadbury Adams North America systems integration project fell behind its timeline when certain tasks were overlooked. The executive sponsor was furious. He said it was unacceptable and that those who were behind would have to stay through the weekend to get caught up. Most team members lived in other parts of the country, so the threat was substantial.

The group got the message and was able to complete the work before the weekend, but his outburst had a lasting impact. Some team members said they were glad it wasn't them who received the public ultimatum, and others kept low profiles for the rest of the project, doing everything they could to avoid a weekend "detention." Anger is a dangerous weapon within a project environment. It can be effective in the short run, but it destroys trust, encourages playing it safe, and motivates people to do anything (even if it's not in the business's interest) to avoid punishment. Healthy confrontation facilitates the sharing of options and ideas; unhealthy confrontation encourages divisiveness and self-preservation.

👍 A new commercial leader joined Cadbury in 2009, just before it faced the fight of its life to remain independent of Kraft Foods. The media followed the battle closely, especially in England, Cadbury's birthplace and biggest market. There was a lot of speculation on how the business would weather the storm, and rumors were rampant. Cadbury described its culture as "performance driven, values led," meaning that actions were driven by a street fighter's belief that the company would always punch above its weight and a higher-order social purpose started by the Cadbury family—"Doing good is good for business." The new leader directed his team to stay focused on winning in the marketplace with customers and consumers, and counseled local sales forces to contribute by delivering superior performance and maintaining professionalism with customers. This leader provided clear direction when the future was unknown and colleagues were vulnerable, and gained respect by doing so.

What Works

- Keep calm. Acts of desperation imply that the situation is out of control and you are not in command of it.

- Be optimistic that the team will solve issues, and keep colleagues focused. Indecision can paralyze a leader and the team. Keeping people busy on doing the most important things will avoid distraction and maintain performance.

- Map out problems and solutions using a simple template (see chart on the next page); this will give you perspective and also test your thinking. Write down what you know and don't know. List what information you have and what you need to get, and include the names of people who can help you find missing information.

- Assign responsibility for gathering data you don't have, and request help from experts who have managed similar challenges.

- Don't blame people for problems, especially in public forums. People watching will fear they may be blamed in the future and will therefore avoid taking risks.

- Hold a debrief meeting after problems are solved. This will allow you to incorporate lessons learned and avoid similar situations from reoccurring.

A change leader is tested most when faced with a challenge that he or she doesn't know how to solve. A positive mind-set, self-confidence, and focused action are necessary, but so is the ability to say, "We've got to step back for a moment."

Problem Overview

Problem: Equipment delivery is delayed by four weeks				
FACTS		**Solution Criteria**	**Possible Solution**	**Pro**	**Con**
What I Know	**What I Don't Know**				
• There is a parts shortage • Existing suppliers are out of stock • Equipment is shipped by ground	• Are there any other suppliers who have the parts? (Eric) • Can equipment be shipped by air? (Ida)	• Cost • Time to implement • Resource use	• Get parts from new supplier	• Quality maintained	• Higher cost • Three-week delay
			• Ship by air	• Quality maintained	• Highest cost • Two-week delay

*http://www.changewithconfidence.com/?page_id=239

CHAPTER 41

How Do I Communicate a Delay in the Project?

Fear and uncertainty thrive on incomplete information.
—John McCoy

COMMUNICATION AROUND PROJECT DELAYS is generally very sensitive. Colleagues may have heard of the problem and the credibility of the team rests on how messages align with what people already unofficially know. People want to know two things: how severe the problem is, and what is being done to correct it—and they will be suspicious if the delay is positioned as a minor setback when something major has gone wrong. Also, colleagues and the leadership team will raise questions about how the project is being managed if an action plan (including who will do what) is not quickly and clearly communicated.

Delays are best discussed according to the chain of command for the project. The executive sponsor needs to be informed first, followed by the rest of the leadership team. You must do this quickly to avoid negative rumors preempting your notification. It is important to be factual, describing the benefits of delaying the project and detailing the impacts to the business. Leaders would rather deal with a setback than a failure, so your decision should be supported. Armed with a recast plan, you will be in a good position to proceed.

Thumbs Down, Thumbs Up

👎 In 1999, Whirlpool Corporation, the household appliance company and maker of the Maytag, KitchenAid, Bauknecht, and Eslabon de Lujo brands, planned a computer system upgrade for the U.S. Labor Day weekend. Three months before the system went live, order-processing red flags were noted. The project team determined that to fix the problems the launch date would need to be delayed by one week. The project manager and his consultant counterpart decided to ignore this recommendation and keep the original date (to preserve the benefits it provided *and* avoid angering executives). The system ran smoothly for the first wave of orders but started to malfunction at the 4,000-order mark, creating havoc with processing. Dealers and retailers missed (or received only partial) shipments for the next four to eight weeks, resulting in many canceled orders, angry dealers, and lost customers. By not communicating risks to the executive sponsor, the project manager and consultant limited the team's ability to manage these risks and exposed the company to financial and reputation damage. Short-term gain led to long-term pain.

👍 A Cadbury Adams USA systems integration project in 2005 was delayed by two months because testing and training could not be completed in time. The president addressed the change at a town hall meeting and in a follow-up letter. First, he thanked everyone involved for their commitment to building a new, combined company. This meant a lot to colleagues, as everyone was working with numerous independent computer systems that weren't connected. Then, he listed the key victories of the project team, especially the successful systems testing and customer engagement.

After congratulating the team and praising what they had achieved, the president addressed the project delay. He started by stating the new launch date, said that more time was needed to install a new warehousing system and additional systems testing and training, and acknowledged that colleagues would be impacted. He closed with a thank-you to all for their adaptability and reaffirmed that the project was a top priority for the business. The transition to the new launch date went smoothly, and the implementation was a success.

What Works

- Build awareness up front that the project will be delayed if all the requirements are not met. If stakeholders are surprised by a delay, they will equate this with mismanagement or failure.

- Fully understand the impacts of the change—timing changes, cross-departmental accommodations, increased costs, and so on.

- Brief the executive sponsor and then the leadership team, and get their approval before any formal communication is sent out.

- Lead with facts and outline the reasons for the delay. If it's due to an incorrect time estimate or a mistake, let the organization know what you have learned from this experience.

- Recommunicate basic information about the project early on:
  - Why the project is necessary for the long-term health of the organization
  - What the project will do
  - How the project will be good for colleagues
  - What the delay is and why it is it happening
  - Vital lessons learned
  - How colleagues will be affected
  - Next steps

- Communicate the risks of not delaying the project.

- Be honest about the reasons for the delay. This will reinforce trust in your leadership (and the project team).

- Create a communications organizer chart to help you gather information you need to communicate in a linear and constructive way (see chart on the next page).

- Avoid assigning blame for the delay. It will embarrass and deflate the identified people and make other team members afraid of making mistakes in the future.

- Do not guarantee there will be no more delays. Doing so might sound reassuring, but your credibility will be compromised if you are wrong.

Communications Organizer

Section	Content
Opening remarks	• How the project will support the organization's strategy and future vision • What benefits it will provide the organization and colleagues • What it has accomplished so far • Thank everyone for their support
Announce delay	• State the initial and new launch date
Rationale for the change	• What are the reasons for the delay? • What are the risks of not delaying the project? • What are the benefits of delaying? • What have we learned from the delay, and how will this help us be successful?
Impact of the change	• List high-level changes that colleagues will experience (e.g., rescheduled training, customer communication requirements, etc.)
Next steps	• List next steps of the team • Highlight follow-up communications
Close	• Reiterate support for the project • Thank everyone again for their support

*http://www.changewithconfidence.com/?page_id=246

Delaying a project is necessary when the core requirements of the plan cannot be fulfilled before the launch date. You need to quickly assess the impacts of a delay, inform leadership, and thoroughly communicate the reasons for postponing the project and what is being done to correct the problem. Doing so effectively and professionally will avoid panic, keep the project team on track, and demonstrate prudent leadership.

CHAPTER 42

How Do I Demonstrate Progress?

Without continual growth and progress, such words as improvement, achievement, and success have no meaning.
—**Benjamin Franklin**

Many a small thing has been made large by the right kind of advertising.
—**Mark Twain**

SOME PROJECT MANAGERS are so buried in the details of their change initiatives that they forget to take the time to communicate progress made. Others communicate progress on technical achievements but don't share successes on preparing people to make the change. The adage "out of sight, out of mind" holds true for change projects. Lack of good news can cause your project to fall off executive and colleague radars and affect the level of compliance to your requests. You need to be the head cheerleader for your project to ensure the organization is always aware of its progress.

Thumbs Down, Thumbs Up

The Harmon Hotel, Spa and Residences in Las Vegas, Nevada, was part of the $9.2-billion CityCenter complex, touted in 2009 as the largest commercial project in U.S. history. The building was marketed as a "towering, shimmering, and glamorous" boutique hotel with a spa and residences. The Lord Norman Foster–designed tower was to be 49 stories high and include 400 hotel rooms, 200 condominiums, and a world-famous Mr. Chow restaurant.

When construction reached the 23rd floor, a structural engineer walked the site and noticed that contractors had incorrectly installed critical steel reinforcement bars on floors 6 to 15, significantly weakening the building's strength. An investigation uncovered that not only had the steel been incorrectly placed but exposed edges of poorly fitted beams had been cut off to hide the errors, further weakening the structure. Third-party construction inspectors had falsified 62 daily progress reports and indicated that construction was in full compliance. County inspectors had failed to spot-check the progress reports and had not pursued unsubmitted floor clearance reports required for authorization to build the next story. The severity of errors required the project to be reduced to 28 floors. Further analysis confirmed that the structure would not be able to withstand earthquakes. Within nine months, one of the tallest buildings in Las Vegas was scheduled for demolition, costing the owners close to $1 billion.

In 2005, Cadbury Adams North America required extensive colleague training to prepare for a new operating software system. The project team and I were concerned because past change projects had suffered from lax training attendance. I highlighted to the leadership team the negative impacts of poor attendance—poor productivity, customer disruption, retraining, and increased project costs. The leadership team agreed to mandate a 100 percent attendance requirement, and each team member agreed to take accountability for their team's participation and to review a weekly training scorecard on attendance statistics by department. Any unapproved absences would be followed up on by a phone call from that colleague's leader.

The scorecard for the first week noted absences in most departments, and one area that had 19 percent no-shows. Leaders made their calls to their team members who didn't attend and within two weeks attendance soared to over 90 percent. We were then able to communicate stellar training statistics as a sign of progress. What gets measured gets done, and leadership oversight and follow-through are the best remedies for poor behavior.

What Works

- Define checkpoints throughout the project. Each checkpoint should have progress accomplishments (percentage of training completed, milestones achieved, etc.). When incorporated into the change plan, this timeline will set expectations for stakeholders.

- Create a one-page dashboard that identifies milestones, issues, wins, and so on, and review it with the leadership team on a regular basis. Establish a "traffic light" system for communicating the status of your project: green "means on track," yellow means "experiencing challenges," and red means "behind or at risk."

Project Dashboard

Week Ending:	August 17	Overall Track Status:	Green
Progress Summary (Top Three Achievements)			
#	**Summary**	**Detail**	
1	Location transition plan	– Agreed on day-one design plan – Communication date of office open house – Completed colleague family photoshoot	
Activities Planned Over Next Reporting Period (Top Three Goals)			
#	**Summary**	**Detail**	
1	Location transition plan	– Identify space conflicts by department – Hold final leadership review meeting to approve furnishings selection – Confirm leadership team participation at office open house	

*http://www.changewithconfidence.com/?page_id=250

- Acknowledge leaders who model new behaviors. Ideally, there will be at least one leader who has made a dramatic change, and this will send a signal to the organization that things are different.

- Request examples of success from every impacted group. (Examples furthest away from the head office are often the most credible, as these groups are more independent.)

- Write articles for your organization's newsletter or create one specifically about your project. Profile colleagues who realize benefits from the project and include pictures of them in their work environments.

Demonstrating progress is an essential element of good project management. Consistent updates on progress remind leaders and colleagues of the work being done, the successes achieved, and the benefits realized once the change is made. They also provide a source of pride for the team for their hard work and achievements.

Once you complete the "Managing Change" phase, you have to "make it stick."

PART 4

Making Change Stick

MANY BIG CHANGE PROJECTS end immediately after the change is made. The project team is disbanded and the leadership moves on to the next big change. This approach assumes the operating business will take on the work of supporting and nurturing the change, still in its infancy. Critical closing procedures such as assigning responsibility for ongoing support, documenting lessons learned, and providing formal recognition of the project team are either done casually or not at all. Too often the operating teams are not sufficiently trained to take on this work, do not have time for it, and are rewarded only for accomplishing other tasks. It's not surprising, then, that these organizations tend to repeat mistakes, have mixed reviews on their capacity for change, and have colleagues who resist joining change project teams.

As a change leader, your role is to ensure that plans are in place so that the change lasts. If this doesn't happen, it's likely that old ways of working will seep back into the business, you will lose some of the benefits of the change, and the project will not be deemed a complete success.

The Plan

CHAPTER 43

How Do I Prevent the Return of Old Ways of Working?

Don't water your weeds.
—**Harvey Mackay**

EVERY BIG CHANGE PROJECT runs the risk that new ways of working won't stick and old ways will reenter the workplace. This can happen immediately after the launch when colleagues are hesitant about taking on new procedures, or later, after they have become used to them. On-site support teams can usually stop old practices from reemerging by guiding people through the new actions, but the most likely time for relapses is after the project team is disbanded and there is no one specifically responsible for monitoring how things get done. Typically, a few people secretly go back to some of their old habits, and if they are not confronted, they will adopt more of them. What might seem like the harmless use of old procedures by some colleagues can quickly turn into an epidemic. Old behaviors can progressively reemerge across the business, creating an inefficient and constantly mutating hybrid organization operating on inconsistent procedures. Competing old and new practices create tensions, and if the situation festers, there will be chaos and the organization will perceive the project as unsuccessful.

Some leaders ignore evidence of the reemergence of old practices, hoping they just will go away. If not addressed, just the opposite happens and people will do more and more things the way they used to. You need to reward new behaviors (and challenge old ones) by building them into ongoing organizational processes, including human resources processes such as performance reviews and colleague rewards.

Thumbs Down, Thumbs Up

👎 The Logistics department of Cadbury Adams Canada was one of the most affected areas of a company-wide software installation in 2005. The warehouse spent months documenting new processes, creating procedural binders, and delivering colleague training. The training had gone well, and early indications of adherence to new ways of working were positive, suggesting that project team support could be removed six weeks after the launch. However, just a few short months later, performance started to drop.

An investigation discovered that supervisors stopped enforcing the new procedures shortly after the project team left. When asked why they did so, they said they found the procedures unnecessarily complex and time-consuming. When colleagues are forced to do things they didn't create (and that don't make sense to them), they will revert to old ways of working as soon as enforcement is removed. The project team would have been more effective had it encouraged candid feedback from warehouse operators. Also, it spent too much time creating binders rather than in face-to-face meetings hammering out practical tools the operators would find useful in the warehouse.

👍 In 1984, Toyota and General Motors created a joint venture called New United Motor Manufacturing Inc. (NUMMI) that transformed an ailing GM factory in Fremont, California, into a highly efficient producer of cars, including the Toyota Corolla and Pontiac Vibe. It was a large facility spanning the equivalent of 88 football fields, and it employed 5,500 people. The partnership provided Toyota with a low-risk entry point into the United States and the chance to test its production system in a new market, while GM stood to benefit from Toyota's ability to profitably make small cars, Toyota's quality systems, and its own opportunity to transform one of its poorest performing sites (and workforces).

Employees were extensively trained in Toyota's "andon" production and management system, which dramatically changed the way supervisors and line operators worked: operators were now obligated to find problems and make improvements, and supervisors were responsible for assisting the operators when problems were found and to stop the production line if quality had been compromised—a far cry from the previous practice of downplaying problems and keeping the line running at all costs. Reward and recognition systems were aligned with the new procedures to acknowledge the focus on quality, support, and ownership. Within one year, the plant was the highest-quality producer for GM.

What Works

- Build the leadership team's awareness of the dangers of old behaviors reemerging, and ask for their commitment to support the new ways. Inertia is a powerful force, and quick intervention is the best way to challenge reemerging status quo behaviors.

- Observe leaders' behaviors for signs of old ways of working. Inertia affects leaders as much as colleagues.

- Remove access to old ways of working so they can't be used.

- Integrate new behaviors into human resources systems, including performance management, leadership training, and orientations for new employees.

- Encourage managers to support the changes by including them in their team's annual performance objectives.

The longer you maintain new ways of working, the more likely it is that they will stick. Developing critical mass will encourage adherence to new behaviors, where momentum is created by the force of the entire organization doing tasks in new ways. Also, rewarding new behaviors and punishing old ones is an effective "carrot and stick" approach to behavior modification. In contrast, allowing old behaviors to coexist with new ones will encourage more colleagues to reject change in favor of what they know best.

CHAPTER 44

How Do I Hand Over Responsibilities to the Business?

Agile project closure is about handing over to the operations team, tidying up loose ends, reviewing the project, celebrating, and going home.

—Steven Thomas

THE PROJECT TEAM NEEDS to transfer its responsibilities to the business operating teams once the new procedures are running smoothly. At this time, the operating teams take over, providing ongoing support activities and controlling future enhancements. A thorough handover process is necessary for a smooth transition between the two teams, and sufficient time for them to discuss project background, new roles, and ongoing needs is necessary.

The period after the project team leaves is delicate because colleagues will still be getting comfortable with new ways of working. They will need continued support to manage tasks and solve issues, and if the handover process is managed well, the operating team members will be properly briefed and have the tools required. If it is done poorly, the change could destabilize, and ongoing benefits may not be realized.

Thumbs Down, Thumbs Up

👎 Bell Canada is Canada's largest telecommunications company. In 1997, Bell World, its retail division, implemented a new IT software system. The project had been twice put on hold and then reactivated months later with a different consulting firm, causing their delays and cost overruns. Many of the franchise store operators put pressure on Bell to quickly complete the installation and reduce costs (that were lowering their profits). The project team responded by rolling off consultants as soon as they had finished their technical work. Some project team members noted that no provision had been made for transferring knowledge from the project team to the internal IT team. A few knowledge-sharing meetings were set up mere days before the project closed. Many of the consultants had already left the project, requiring additional discussions to be held by phone in the evenings. Problems arose after the launch when system interfaces didn't work properly and the consultants who had designed them had moved on. Also, there was a lack of understanding about how the system had been configured, and this made modifications difficult. It took many months for the business to realize the full benefits of the new system.

👍 With mines in three continents, Cameco is one of the world's largest uranium producers. In the planning phase of a new operating system project in 1996, it became clear that most project team roles would be filled by external consultants, and the leadership team realized that this resourcing model created the risk of a large knowledge gap: if the consultants couldn't sufficiently transfer their knowledge, the information would be lost or consultant contracts would need to be extended, resulting in significant additional costs.

Knowledge transition plans were created for each consultant to manage his or her information transfer throughout the project. Each plan was co-owned by a project or IT colleague and a consultant. The process included identifying what knowledge had to be transitioned, who needed to receive it, and how that transition would occur. The plan also incorporated training and support to facilitate the exchanges, and knowledge transfer checkpoints were defined with clear requirements. All transition plans were completed successfully. Project knowledge was transferred according to checkpoint specifications, and consultants finished their work on schedule.

What Works

- Appoint people responsible for new processes and systems at the beginning of the project, and invite them to checkpoint meetings to build their awareness of project details.

- Create a project handover plan to ensure that the colleagues with new responsibilities are properly briefed, and include in it a checklist itemizing the steps for completing a thorough transition. Track the plan's completion.

Project Handover Checklist

Tasks	☑
Schedule handover meeting	☐
Compile documentation	☐
Send out agenda and read in advance of the meeting	☐
Hold the meeting	☐
Complete follow-up tasks	☐
Distribute documentation CDs	☐
Notify managers of handover completion	☐

*http://www.changewithconfidence.com/?page_id=258

- Compile key project documents, with short executive summaries for each.

- Create a project closure document to outline original parameters and changes made to them—include results, lessons learned, and ongoing support requirements.

- Schedule a project handover meeting to provide the new process and systems owners with the information they will need. The roles and responsibilities section provides team members with an opportunity to share thoughts on how to best manage their new responsibilities and share information on specific challenges.

Project Handover Meeting Agenda

Agenda
Objectives
Review project closure document
– Project overview: objectives, outcomes/deliverables (including measurements)
– Project results
– Lessons learned
– Ongoing support: owners and activities
– Roles and responsibilities overview
– Documentation overview
– Questions and answers period
– Closing comments

*http://www.changewithconfidence.com/?page_id=260

- Send project materials in advance of the handover meeting, ask new owners to review them, and build new owner responsibilities into their annual objectives.

- Notify the new owners' managers that the handover activities are completed. This will signify that accountabilities have been transferred.

A project team's effectiveness in transferring responsibilities to operating teams often dictates the level of long-term adoption of new ways of working. A thorough handover process ensures that new owners of post-launch responsibilities have the knowledge, tools, and confidence to complete their mandate. Also, when done well, the two teams form a relationship that encourages ongoing communication and assistance. Effective transfers require early planning, thorough documentation, and commitment from all parties.

CHAPTER 45

How Do I Record Lessons Learned?

The error of the past is the wisdom and success of the future.
—Dale E. Turner

PROJECT TEAM MEMBERS AND LEADERS don't always record or share lessons learned because there are few rewards for doing so. At the end of a project, energy is focused on deliverables and tying up loose ends. Many leaders don't request a thorough review because they have already redirected their attention to other active projects, and fighting new battles is more pressing than documenting old ones. Others are not keen to reveal mistakes for fear they will overshadow the project's accomplishments. Still others don't see negative consequences arising from ignoring lessons learned and therefore do not take action.

The project manager needs to drive the process of recording and sharing knowledge so that future projects can benefit from it. Understanding lessons learned helps build change capacity and skill, and dramatically improves organizational knowledge on how projects work within a certain culture. Experience is the best teacher: future project roadblocks will be eliminated by altering past approaches, whereas repeating past mistakes will cause additional costs, delays, and damage to customer and supplier relationships. Also, a thorough review of lessons learned will demonstrate your leadership capability. Understanding the variables of the project and how you can secure greater performance is a core leadership trait.

Thumbs Down, Thumbs Up

As a Cadbury Adams systems integration was winding down in 2005, most project team members already had been reassigned, and contractors had left the business. I was keen to get the lessons learned from the project team members before the project completely closed. A review session was organized and most of the remaining team members attended by phone or in person. A lessons learned document was created based on everyone's feedback.

I was unable to get time on a leadership team meeting agenda to review the lessons learned summary so decided to circulate the document to the executive. My fears were that they would not read it because the review session hadn't been positioned as important at the beginning of the project, and that most of the leaders didn't see it as a key driver of future business performance. Establishing the importance of project review sessions and scheduling them into meeting calendars is the best way to ensure they are taken seriously and done well.

In 2010, during the planning phase of the Kraft-Cadbury merger, the global change leaders from both organizations agreed that the integration would be guided by lessons from past integrations. They each compiled summaries from their respective organizations, and these were used to develop a change management framework for the merger. Beyond benefiting from the past experiences, the knowledge that both company's lessons learned were being used signaled to Cadbury colleagues that their new employer valued their input. The partnership between change leaders was extended to all regional and national division teams, which further reinforced the collaborative nature of the integration. At the end of the merger, an in-depth lessons learned summary was added to the company's knowledge about managing change.

What Works

- Add a lessons learned activity to your project plan. Include stakeholder interviews and impacted-groups and project-team focus groups.

- Keep an ongoing log of lessons learned (see chart on next page). Capturing them in real time will ensure you don't forget key lessons and make it easier to create a summary at the end of the project. Details, especially on the human aspects of stakeholder influence and team management, hold the most valuable lessons.

- Create a simple "what worked" and "what could have been done better" chart to document lessons learned in a format easy to present to stakeholders.

- Interview all stakeholders and project team members, asking them the following questions:

  - What worked well?

  - What didn't work well?

  - What was difficult to accomplish?

  - What would you do differently?

  - Were there any surprises during the project? How could they have been avoided?

- Review the lessons learned summary with the project team to check for accuracy and completeness before sharing it with the leadership team.

- Create a project overview CD that includes key documents (project plan, communications, updates, lessons learned, etc.). Distribute it to the leadership team, key stakeholders, and project team members.

The capturing and reviewing of lessons learned needs to be valued by project and leadership teams. Organizations that record and provide access to their lessons learned ensure that future big change projects repeat successful practices and avoid mistakes. This knowledge helps build capabilities to manage change successfully and minimize disruptions to the business.

Lessons Learned Summary

Area	What Worked?	What Could Have Been Done Better?
Governance	• Guiding principles helped prioritize work	• Clearer communication of guiding principles at the project kickoff would have better aligned stakeholders
Stakeholder engagement	• Scheduled meetings with stakeholders ensured they were informed and provided forums to air concerns	
Change management	• Appointing local change representatives facilitated two-way information sharing	• Some representatives did not have the authority or skills to influence local leaders
Communication	• Electronic and face-to-face communications worked well	• Most remote locations did not hold consistent feedback sessions
Tools	• The tools were easy to use	
Risk management	• Each impacted area completed a thorough risk analysis, including contingency plans	• The plans were not effectively communicated to teams—this was apparent when a risk materialized and it was unclear who was responsible for fixing it
Resourcing	• There were sufficient resources allocated to the project	• Team member attrition was higher than anticipated due to career path considerations
Consultant partnership	• The initial planning phase was well executed	• A couple of team members were moved to other assignments, requiring additional efforts to orient new members

CHAPTER 46

How Do I Reenter the Business?

Begin with the end in mind.
—**Stephen Covey**

YOU NEED TO START THINKING OF REENTERING the business before you begin your project role. Some people assume that the organization will take care of them and that finding a good role is not their responsibility because they have worked hard and deserve one as a reward. Although an organization's intentions might be good, it doesn't always work out that way. Departments are rarely the same after a big change project: they restructure, people take on new roles or leave, and new priorities are set. Also, your former role might have been reassigned or its responsibilities redistributed to other team members. The odds are that you will be taking on a new role.

The good news is that your efforts to influence your next role will be noticed because most people don't think about doing so. You'll be able to position yourself for a good next role by staying in contact with your former team and developing a new network of cross-departmental team members from the project. This will allow you to maximize the experiences provided by the big change project and become more marketable to the operating business.

Thumbs Down, Thumbs Up

While working on the Cadbury and Adams merger in 2003, the Cadbury Americas Region Human Resources Team, of which I was a member, was having a meeting in Miami. It was a new team made up of former Cadbury and Adams members, and this would be their first face-to-face meeting. The timing couldn't have been worse, as the project integration group was working night and day toward a big deadline. Initially, my two change leaders and I agreed not to go to the meeting so we could focus on our project duties, but we quickly changed our minds upon seeing the agenda. It included a full-day planning session on determining the next year's initiatives. By then the merger would be over, and we feared that being "out of sight and out of mind" could result in us being left out in the cold, with no jobs to go back to. We booked a 24-hour trip to attend the planning meeting. It was a whirlwind journey that probably had little impact on our future roles, but being there made us feel more secure in a time of uncertainty. Without a defined reentry plan, people usually fear the worst and act accordingly. In this case, costs included loss of focus, lost productivity and greater stress.

The National Health Services of England is the oldest publicly funded healthcare system in the world. Kirklees Primary Care Trust, a local affiliate providing services to a community of 400,000, instituted a secondment system to ensure that the organization's and employees' interests would be met. The former and new managers were given joint responsibility for the secondment. They developed agreements for each team member, including performance objectives, role descriptions, length of assignments (maximum two years), and personal development plans. The former department manager organized a "keep in touch" program before the assignment started to maintain connections between employees and their departments. It included update meetings to attend, documents to be shared, and a schedule of check-in visits. Well before the end of the assignment, the two managers evaluated progress on each team member's development plan and manage his or her reentry back into the business. A disciplined and well-publicized secondment process helps ensure that project team members stay connected with the business and are supported through their reentry process.

What Works

- Meet monthly with your former manager throughout the project. He or she can update you on business developments, and you can share how you are building new capabilities and experience.

- Learn about other areas of the business. Projects usually have cross-departmental elements that provide excellent opportunities to expand your network and uncover future job prospects.

- Stay in contact with your former team. Colleagues tend to lose touch once they start a project.

- Request that your former manager attend project performance review meetings.

- Maintain a positive and professional disposition during the project. (Some people can't seem to control their behavior when under stress then wonder why it is difficult to reenter the operating business.)

- Meet with your Human Resources representative two months before the project ends to get his or her perspective on job opportunities.

- Avoid talking about your next role with the project team. It will be perceived that you have checked out of the project.

Big change projects provide excellent opportunities to build capabilities, expand your knowledge of the business, and expand your personal network. To fully capitalize on these benefits you need to plan your reentry into the business so that your name remains top-of-mind and you maximize the number of future roles to be considered for. To some colleagues, it might seem like you never left business operations.

Resources

CHAPTER 47

How Do I Plan for Post-Launch Support?

Focusing solely on [the] launch is akin to planning for the wedding, rather than the marriage.

—Paul Scherer

THE "MAKING CHANGE STICK" PHASE typically has the least planning and resources applied to it. Once the launch is complete and things appear stable, many organizations view the project as done, and scale back support even though the new ways of working are still fresh. There is a big difference between a change that has been launched and one that has been adopted. When a big change is launched, people are in an incubator filled with support, measurement tools, and analysis, but it has only been fully adopted when colleagues habitually use the new ways of working. This transition can take months, but once it happens, the full benefits of the change will be realized. You need to ensure that sufficient post-launch support is available until the change is fully adopted and success is confirmed.

Thumbs Down, Thumbs Up

In 2007, the State of Idaho's Department of Health and Welfare entered into a $106 million contract with Unisys to build (and operate until 2014) an IT system to automate Medicaid claims payments to health care providers.

Importantly, Unisys's health IT division (including this contract) was sold to Molina Healthcare Inc. prior to the launch date.

The system had not met pretesting standards when it was launched in June 2010. Errors were noticed immediately, and the call center set up for post-launch support was overloaded. Health care providers called to report delayed and inaccurate payments, but 50 percent of them hung up because of long wait times (more than 35 minutes on average). Over 240 system defects were documented (28 coded severe, about 200 major, and 12 minor). A month after the launch, staff was increased by 85 percent.

Some claims were rejected because the health care providing companies were entered incorrectly in the system. Some had received training on the new system six months prior to the launch (and there was no post-launch training anticipated or provided). "Triage teams" were formed to solve the highest priority issues, but only the providers with these problems received progress notifications, and 58,400 claims were still backlogged by February 2012. Furthermore, some issues were recorded as being resolved when either they were still outstanding or the "resolution" created other system problems.

Post-launch reporting was another oversight. Backlogged claims were not tracked until September, so there was no overall assessment of performance. Molina Healthcare reported weekly on claims that had been paid or denied but did not report on claims that had been paid incorrectly, which made the situation seem better than it was. An internal audit was ordered in March 2011. It provided recommendations for future system installations, which Molina Healthcare generally agreed with. The Department of Health and Welfare was forced to authorize over $117 million in advances to providers until errors could be corrected.

In 2007, after Cadbury Adams Canada's successful launch of a new commercial software program, a colleague who had provided launch assistance was given the role of ongoing trainer. He coordinated and led training sessions in addition to his regular duties and became the go-to person whenever staff had problems. He was selected for a more senior role on the next systems project.

Experts are often created during a big change project, and finding ways to use these capabilities after the project closes will greatly increase the probability that new ways of working will stick. Also, doing so rewards colleagues who have helped build the business.

What Works

Content

- Set a concrete end date for the project. At this time, the project team will officially disband and ongoing accountabilities will shift to colleagues in the business. Phased in roll-offs may be more practical, but they tend to signal an early end to the project, encouraging team members to focus on future roles instead of completing the project.

- Negotiate for at least six weeks of post-launch support. Studies suggest that it takes from 45 to 90 days for new behaviors to become habitual.

- Request project team members take on post-launch duties. They are the most knowledgeable and have an emotional attachment to the new ways of working.

- Develop an ongoing training strategy. New or struggling colleagues will need to receive training on the new systems and processes. You'll need to define who will do the training and build these responsibilities into their work plans.

- Assign people responsibility for each new process. This will ensure accountability for ongoing maintenance, upgrades, and education—all necessary, especially in regard to new software packages.

- Request that an influential manager be responsible for documenting ongoing issues and benefits of the change. Someone who doesn't want to see the project backtrack is ideal because he or she will do so thoroughly and enthusiastically.

- Communicate to the organization who will be accountable for achieving and tracking ongoing benefits to the business.

Process

- Discuss post-launch support at least one month before the activation date. If you agree on resources too early, circumstances may change as assigned people leave the business—for example, if you discuss it too late, there may be insufficient resources to manage activities.

- Create a post-launch resource plan for all new processes and systems (see chart on the next page). This will help ensure that new ways of working are followed and modifications made.

- Get sign-off for the post-launch plan as part of the overall project plan.

It takes time and dedicated support for colleagues to fully adopt a big change. People will need job aids and other support materials for weeks (or longer) after the launch until they become familiar with their new rituals. Ideally, support resources are made available until the new ways of working become ingrained in daily routines. It is less risky to plan thoroughly for post-launch support than to eliminate resources and scramble to add them if the change doesn't stick.

Post-Launch Resource Plan

Finance System	Colleague	Process Owner (approver of updates)	Training	Measurement
		• Oversee process • Approve updates	• Maintain training materials • Deliver training • Coordinate sessions	• Collect data • Conduct analysis • Report monthly
Cognos	Raj	✓		
	Shari		✓	✓
Hyperion	Tony	✓	✓	✓
	Kevin		✓	

CHAPTER 48

How Do I Reward the Team?

The first responsibility of a leader is to define reality.
The last is to say thank you.

—Max De Pree

LEADERS AND COLLEAGUES TEND TO REMEMBER two parts of a project most vividly: the beginning and the end. The middle is a gray area that is usually forgotten unless something major went wrong. How you close a project will significantly influence team members' perceptions of how they were treated while working on it *and* how they will feel working on future projects. People have a need to be recognized for their commitment and engagement, and by doing so you not only acknowledge their hard work but encourage similar efforts in the future.

There are many ways to acknowledge team members for their hard work. Providing a celebratory final event helps them close the project before moving on to their next roles. It will give team members the opportunity to share stories and acknowledge achievements, and allow people to positively frame their experiences, even if the project was not completely successful. Also, gift giving is an effective way to recognize colleagues who have worked hard to make it a success. Tangible rewards have value in and of themselves and are sources of bragging rights to peers, family, and friends.

Thumbs Down, Thumbs Up

By 2003, a quality-improvement project had been underway at Cadbury Trebor Allan for over a year, but the desired behavioral changes hadn't improved performance. A new leader was brought in to turn the business around. He didn't support continuing the initiative, preferring to make much smaller and simpler process changes. The project was abandoned and team members reassigned. There was no project wrap-up for the work that had been done because the new leader felt that such acknowledgment would reward the organization's poor performance.

The project team members felt exhausted and unappreciated. Some felt "ripped off" and lacked passion about the new drive for better results. Some were wary about joining the next culture project a few years later. People have good memories; they remember how they are treated and will refer back to past experiences before signing up for new opportunities. The new leader should have acknowledged past efforts and then called on these people to help him make the new direction successful. As the project manager, I should have privately rewarded the team members. By not doing either of these things, we reinforced the adage that, "What doesn't get rewarded rarely gets done again."

St Marys Cement is a leading manufacturer of cement (and related construction products) that supplies the U.S. and Canadian markets. In 2000, it needed to transfer its business data to a new IT system because its current system had become inoperable. The project team worked night and day to shorten the project timeline to reduce risk to the business. It was able to set up the new computer system and transfer all data files in only five months, a record for this type of project.

The company invested part of the project cost savings into rewarding the team. It was given a large celebration where the project manager profiled each member's contributions (with real-life examples of what they did). Also, every team member was given a personalized family retreat vacation to acknowledge the personal sacrifices made to achieve the early launch. The leadership team also recommended the consulting company's team for a customer service award, which it won.

What Works

- Hold a final dinner meeting for the project team to acknowledge the hard work of the team.

- Ask the leader of the company or the executive sponsor to attend the dinner, a signal to all employees that the project is important and the team's efforts valued.

- Give the team a present that is a tangible symbol of the initiative.

- Take pictures of the recognition meeting and give them to all team members.

- Help team members transition back to operating roles. You need to make this a priority because it is the right thing to do, and because people will not want to leave their operational roles in the future if colleagues have been penalized for doing so.

People seek to find meaning in their work, and one of the ways they do so is through the praise and recognition they receive. Whether it is a personal thank-you from a respected leader or a gift they wouldn't buy for themselves, the acknowledgment rewards people for their efforts, and acknowledged efforts inspire future effort and performance.

Getting Results

CHAPTER 49

How Do I Keep the Change Alive?

Great things are done by a series of small things brought together.
—Vincent van Gogh

AFTER THE PROJECT HAS BEEN IMPLEMENTED, colleagues will naturally identify modifications to improve processes and procedures. They may, however, not push to have them put in place, being too busy to do so or assuming someone else will be doing it.

An effective way of keeping the change alive is to determine what needs fixing or enhancing so that the change works for colleagues and the project realizes its intended benefits (or even uncovers new benefits) and full potential. Each modification should make colleagues' lives easier and improve effectiveness, so the more you can identify, the better the change will be. (Left unfixed, they will become irritants to colleagues and will negatively influence their perceptions of the change.) Once identified and validated, they need to be incorporated into the work plans of the respective teams to ensure they get done. This will improve productivity, increase ownership of the new ways of working, make colleagues' roles easier, and help keep the change active.

Thumbs Down, Thumbs Up

Overstock.com, an online retailer, installed a new computer system in 2005. The CEO mandated a shorter project timeline than the consultants recommended so that the system would be up and running before the high-traffic Christmas season. The new system did not work properly when it was launched—orders couldn't be tracked or confirmed—and the system had to be shut down for a week. It was a disaster. One customer received only two of seven MP3 players he ordered and got bizarre responses from the Customer Service department when he called for help: it was impossible, he was told, that the box didn't have the items; an order trace was in progress (from a system that was not working); the missing goods was a shipping partner's fault; he would get a refund (which didn't happen); and the company could prove that it sent all seven MP3 players to him. The CEO admitted the company had experienced more trouble than expected after the launch but said there was no influx in complaints following the installation of the new system. He was wrong.

In 2006, the CEO wrote to shareholders admitting that "the IT problem that developed last September . . . has had lingering effects that ran well into this year."[1] Financial reports were refiled to correct how freight costs had been recorded. In 2007, the CEO said, "It has taken an enormous amount of work to recover but our operations and infrastructure are now healthy and strong."[2] In 2008, Overstock.com executives announced they were adjusting earnings again from 2003 onward in order to correct another accounting error in the new systems (that resulted in a $12.9 million reduction in revenue and $10.3 million increase in net losses). The CEO explained: "When we upgraded our system, we didn't hook up some of the accounting wiring; however, we thought we had manual fixes in place. We've since found that these manual fixes missed a few of the unhooked wires."[3] Overstock.com recorded its first "real" annual profit in 2010.

In 2009, Coca-Cola, the largest manufacturer, distributor, and marketer of nonalcoholic beverages in the world, embarked on a massive global outsourcing project for its human resources services. The new service delivery model would improve efficiency (to meet peer company standards), globally align processes, and decrease costs. After each of four regional launches, the project team monitored adoption of new ways of working, audited procedures, and simplified (and improved) colleague relations with the external partner to ensure the new system worked well.

Colleagues were encouraged to identify improvements to the system, which were piloted in small areas, studied and optimized, and then rolled out to all 102 national divisions. The company and its partner then implemented a process of continuous improvement to capture future opportunities for augmenting ways of working and increasing performance.

What Works

- Ask colleagues what changes they would make to improve ways of working. They will have clear opinions based on their day-to-day experiences.

- Schedule face-to-face "What's working? What's not?" meetings to assess how the new ways of working are being adopted and which elements need modification. In-person meetings maximize the number of inputs received and allow you to ask questions on unclear comments. Agendas that start with general high-level questions and move to more specific explorations tend to work well. Send out invites before you launch the change so that colleagues are prepared to give feedback.

Post-Launch Feedback Meeting Agenda

Agenda
Welcome and thank-you
Activity: What is working well (processes, relationships, systems)?
Activity: What could be working better (processes, relationships, systems)?
Activity: How would you improve what could be working better?
What benefits are you seeing now?
What benefits do you foresee in the future?
Open forum: Anything else to share?
Closing comments and thank-you

*http://www.changewithconfidence.com/?page_id=276

- Asking people to write out their comments under the headings of "Process," "Relationships," and "Systems" is an effective way to categorize feedback. Similar comments can be grouped together and explored in more detail.

- Invite cross-departmental colleagues to ensure processes are working well between teams.

- Commit to updating colleagues who attend feedback sessions. This courtesy will build an ongoing feedback community that will enable continuous improvement.

- Share recommendations with the leadership team, and ask for the good ones to be formally approved.

- Set up ongoing user groups to manage challenges, record wins, and recommend upgrades. Support is required to build a community of like-minded colleagues keen to get the most out of their systems.

People who are using the new ways of working are your main source of improvement ideas. They know their jobs and what needs to happen to be effective and efficient. You must provide them with opportunities to share what works and what doesn't, and listen carefully to their recommendations. Many of them will be practical and cost effective. Encouraging feedback and quickly acting on suggestions will motivate people to stick with new procedures.

CHAPTER 50

How Do I Show that the Project Was a Success?

No way of thinking or doing, however ancient, can be
trusted without proof.

—Henry David Thoreau

THERE ARE MANY CREDIBLE WAYS TO SHED light on a project team's performance, but when presenting results it is best to start with the measurements agreed to at the outset. Facts and data outlining before and after results are the best evidence of goal achievement. Then, you can share additional evidence that speaks to the quality and effectiveness of your team's work. Verbal testimonials from leaders and colleagues also are effective, but without fact-based documentation you run the risk that these general perceptions may change over time, which can change how the project is viewed.

Conducting a formal post-project review allows you to remind leaders of the agreed-upon outcomes and provide evidence that you have achieved them. This will be the first meeting where you can tell the complete story of your project. The numbers will demonstrate performance, and your commentary will reflect the challenges you faced and your team's abilities to overcome them. Once the results have been acknowledged, you can officially close the project and enjoy the acknowledgments the team deserves.

Thumbs Down, Thumbs Up

In 2003, the U.S. Air Force and Department of Defense commissioned an 800,000-square-foot hotel, mall, and community center complex at the Ramstein Air Base in Germany, the largest facility ever built by these organizations. In 2007, the Air Force did a status check on the project after it had fallen two years behind schedule and was over budget. The original cost estimate was $150 million, but a revised forecast of $200 million was given to the task force, though it did not cover the additional costs of reinstalling faulty construction. The project won the 2006 Air Force Design Award for its environmentally friendly, one-of-a-kind green roof and glass domes, but the roof had massive leaks and repair costs were unclear as the roof contractor had gone bankrupt. Half of the roof would have to be replaced in 2008 at a cost of $10 million.

Neither the project team nor the German government construction agency responsible for managing all foreign military projects, LBB-Kaiserslautern, could provide a completion date. It was difficult to gain information because the LBB-Kaiserslautern project managers had been replaced (and were under criminal investigation for fraud), the construction management contractor had been fired, and the senior Air Force civilian working on the project had resigned. Also, documentation was difficult to review because LBB-Kaiserslautern did not maintain an updated construction schedule to coordinate work between contractors. The project was completed in 2009, more than three years behind the original schedule.

At the end of the formal Kraft-Cadbury integration project in 2010, a review meeting was held with the global Human Resources leadership team. The change leaders presented a project review document that had been circulated prior to the meeting. Accomplishments and lessons learned were discussed with input from the regional leaders, as was the need for additional change management support. The regional leaders unanimously agreed that no further central support was required. The document was distributed to all major national divisions, confirming that their feedback had been included.

Consensus on your project's success based on agreed-upon measurements is important because it signifies that all stakeholders agree with the value it has provided. If they aren't aligned, your project will not be widely acknowledged or referenced in the future. The most powerful signs of success are those coming from the people who are living with the change, and including their feedback builds a credible view of the benefits delivered.

What Works

- Hold a final leadership team project review meeting to demonstrate the project's achievements based on preset measurements. The most effective review meetings are short and tight, conveying momentum and professionalism.

Project Closure Meeting Agenda

Agenda
Project overview: objectives, outcomes/deliverables (including measurements)
Project results: metrics review, testimonials, and anecdotes
Lessons learned: What worked and what could have been done better?
Ongoing support and benefits tracking: owners and activities
Closing comments

*http://www.changewithconfidence.com/?page_id=280

- Create an end-of-project review document that provides an overview of the project—its objectives, accomplishments, and lessons learned—and schedule short meetings with all stakeholders not present at the leadership meeting to review project results.

- Ensure that high-level results are communicated to the business. This provides an opportunity for colleagues to celebrate success and reaffirms that change projects are necessary to achieve higher performance.

- Submit your project to an industry awards program. This will provide exposure for your organization and garner external validation of your team's accomplishments.

Facts and data are critical to showing that your project is a success, but the story behind the success will be remembered long after the numbers are forgotten. Spend time writing the story of your project and be sure to include descriptive details of challenges and the steps taken to overcome them. Make sure your project's success is broadcast across the organization: it is good for morale and provides another opportunity for your team (and you) to be recognized. After all the hours, days, weeks, and months of hard work, it is time to celebrate.

AFTERWORD

MOST CHANGE LEADERS let out a huge sigh of relief when a big project closes. But, in time, a certain quiet comes over them: something exciting, challenging, and meaningful has come to an end. I remember the organizer of the 1984 Los Angeles Olympics sailing competition telling me that he sat in the middle of the command center and wept when the post-event party was over.

At the end of your big change project, you will have many stories to tell about stepping into the unknown and overcoming barriers, or making mistakes that you have learned from and will never make again. You'll also have stories about the relationships you formed and the victories you shared. These rich experiences are what *Change with Confidence* is all about—the courage to move an organization, and its colleagues, into the future. It's difficult at times, even hellish, but in this world big change projects are almost always necessary to improve your organization's health and performance, and being involved, being stuck in the muck and mud of it all, is exhilarating.

I hope this book demonstrates that the best strategy for adopting big changes is to answer the questions around them well and to provide the people who are changing course with everything they need to take on new ways of working—including respect, encouragement, information, tools, and the opportunity to shape the change to fit their environment. They ultimately decide whether or not the change will stick, and when it does, the organization will gain the full benefits of your project.

No two change projects are exactly alike, but they all share similar characteristics and patterns. As a change leader, it is up to you to share your change experiences, and the more you can share your stories and lessons learned, the better equipped your colleagues will be at managing future big changes.

It has been a year since my last big change project and I miss the feeling of being a change leader, the dynamism of the extended moment. I knew that if I stayed at Kraft there would be fascinating projects to dive into, but I had been a global commuter for nine years and the effects were starting to show, on both me and my family. At the beginning of the Kraft and Cadbury integration, I picked up my son Charlie from school (on a rare day I was home). He was visibly upset, and when I asked him why he said that his teacher had announced two tests for the following day on top of a major assignment being due. I said, "Let's organize what you have to do. I am here for you for the next 30 minutes before I have to go to the airport." He gave me a look that I will never forget—I was failing my son. I realized I needed to make a big personal change for Charlie; our oldest son, Sam; my wife, Barb; and me. It was time to come home to Toronto and start something new. I met with the Human Resources integration leader and told him that I would be leaving Kraft when the project was over (and promised to stay until then). I ended up staying a few months after the integration, before starting to write this book.

Within a week of leaving Kraft, I dove into writing and, perhaps somehow related, started training for my first marathon. My change project was off to a good start. Once I completed the last draft of *Change with Confidence*, I started a consulting company of the same name. I love change management and it is thrilling be back in the action, helping leaders and their teams build confidence by helping to answer the questions that can make them successful.

Change projects are challenging. They test your abilities and composure as you ride the roller coaster from where an organization is to where it needs to go. Shortly after successfully closing your project, you might wonder when you will next get the opportunity to ride again. I know I did.

ACKNOWLEDGMENTS

MY HEARTFELT THANKS goes to my amazing wife, Barb, and sons, Sam and Charlie. Your love, encouragement, and advice have been tremendous. Also, warm thanks to my personal editor, Ken Alexander, who is responsible for transforming the book I intended to write into the book that it could be. Seldom are we lucky enough to meet individuals capable of rewiring how we think, and Ken is one of those people for me. Your wisdom and caring have made me a better writer, and I will always be grateful to you for this.

I feel privileged to be working with a tremendous team at Wiley, led by my Executive Editor, Karen Milner, who started our great partnership. My appreciation extends to all Wiley team members who have helped in their own special ways: Deborah Guichelaar, Jeremy Hanson-Finger, Josie Krysiak, Elizabeth McCurdy, John Nixon, Terry Palmer, Judith Phillips, Kim Rossetti, Pam Vokey, Lucas Wilk, and Brian Will.

Thank you to all of my friends and other family members for your keen interest and encouragement along the way. Four friends in particular made numerous suggestions that found their way into this book and provided me with terrific guidance every step of the way. Dan Azoulay, an author and professor, provided a window for me to see the responsibilities of an author and the fortitude to be my best; Melodie Barnett, communicator and change leader, kept me honest and made sure I spoke the full truth; John Bradley, an author and facilitator, pulled me from the weeds and helped me see the big picture; and Tim Morton, change leader, reinforced the need for integrity and courage through all aspects of change.

I would also like to thank the following, all of whom have contributed to this book: Darren Ashby, Raya Azoulay, Peter Babiak, Eric Beaudan, Debbie Bliss, Don Buckley, Ellen Buckley, Jim Buckley, Steve Buckley, Linda Cattelan, Doug Crosbie, Emanuel Galvert, Kate Georgiades, Luisa Girotto, Misha Glouberman, Stewart Hardacre, Tim Hopson, Shari Hosaki, Anthony Hunt, Krishan Jayatunge, Anne Kemp, Ida Kofoed, Maria Lickert, Jan Lowenthal, Paula Lytwn, Diane Marchesello, Roger Martin, Chuck McVinney, Dave Morel, David Neal, Bob Noftall, Elaine Oh, Kevin O'Leary, Mark O'Reily, Marlene Pape, Kevin Power, Bharat Puri, Kathy Repa, Andrea Robottom, Matt Ross, Ajey Sabharwal, Raj Sabharwal, Anne Sawbridge, Gail Severini, Eric Simpson, Dana Stevens, Paul Tepperman, David Thompson, Marge Watters, Richard Wilding, Brad Wilson, Anna Zaltz, and Joel Zelikovitz. As friends, current and former colleagues, and business professionals, your generosity and insights remain an inspiration.

NOTES

Preface

1. Haspeslagh, P., Noda, T., Noda, T., Boulos, F. (2001, July-August) "Managing for Value: It's Not Just About the Numbers", *Harvard Business Review*, Vol. 79, No. 7, p. 54–73

Chapter 1

1. Ashkenas, R., Francis, S., Heinick, R. (2011, July-August) "The Merger Dividend", *Harvard Business Review*, p. 130

Chapter 12

1. Krigsman, M. (2009, January 28) "Angst in Oak Park Over Failed PeopleSoft Project", IT Project Failures Blog, *ZDNet.com*, http://www.zdnet.com/blog/projectfailures/angst-in-oak-park-over-failed-peoplesoft-project/1358
2. Wilson-Bett, W. (2006, November 6) Cadbury Schweppes Winning Choices Mastery Forum, London, England

Chapter 14

1. (2008, March 14) "Queen Opens New Heathrow Terminal", *BBC News*, http://news.bbc.co.uk/2/hi/uk_news/7294618.stm
2. Krigsman, M. (2008, April 7) "IT Failure at Heathrow T5: What Really Happened", IT Project Failures Blog, *ZDNet.com*, http://www.zdnet.com/blog/projectfailures/it-failure-at-heathrow-t5-what-really-happened/681

Chapter 18

1. Strbac S. (2006) "The Staffing Process for Product Development Projects: A case study at 3P, Volvo AB", Master's Thesis, Chalmers University of Technology, Northumbria University, Göteborg, Sweden, p. 31

Chapter 19

1. County of Marin's complaint against Deloitte Consulting LLP, Superior Court of California, May 28, 2010, http://www.scribd.com/doc/32419050/Marin-County-complaint-against-Deloitte-Consulting-on-failed-SAP-project
2. Krigsman, M. (2010, March 31) "Marin County Claims Racketeering Against Deloitte and SAP, Part One", IT Project Failures Blog, *ZDNet.com*, http://www.zdnet.com/blog/projectfailures/marin-county-claims-racketeering-against-deloitte-and-sap-part-one/12749

Chapter 31

1. Goldstein, H. (2005, September) "Who Killed the Virtual Case File?", *IEEE Spectrum*, http://spectrum.ieee.org/computing/software/who-killed-the-virtual-case-file
2. Hayes, F. (2005, May 30) "FBI on the Move", *Computerworld*, http://www.computerworld.com/s/article/102080/FBI_on_the_Move

Chapter 35

1. (2012, May 12) "Loblaw Companies Limited Reports 2012 First Quarter Results", *Loblaw Companies Limited*, http://www.loblaw.ca/English/Media-Centre/news-releases/news-release-details/2012/Loblaw-Companies-Limited-Reports-2012-First-Quarter-Results11129252/default.aspx
2. Dupain, W. (2009, June) "Managing Change in the 21st Century: The Journey Towards the New World of Work", Master's Thesis, RSM Erasmus University, Rotterdam, the Netherlands
3. Ibid.
4. Hirt, M., van der Meer, H. (2012, October 11) "How Microsoft Netherlands Reinvented the Way of Work (Really)", *Management Innovation Exchange*, http://www.managementexchange.com/story/microsoft-netherlands

Chapter 36

1. Mombourquette, A. (2011, October 31) "Readers Pretty Well in Tune: Canada Post, Smarten Up", *The Chronicle Herald*, http://thechronicleherald.ca/hcw/28254-readers-pretty-well-tune-canada-post-smarten

2. Walker, B. (2012, May) "The Last Post", *The Walrus*, p. 51

3. Mombourquette, A. (2011, October 20) "Were Canada Post workers forgotten in 'transformation'?", *The Chronicle Herald*, http://thechronicleherald.ca/hcw/26268-were-canada-post-workers-forgotten-transformation

Chapter 39

1. "Millennium Exhibition—The New Millennium Experience", *Greenwich* 2000 http:// greenwich2000.co.uk/millennium/experience/company.htm

Chapter 49

1. Vance, A. (2006, November 7) "Overstock.com Overflops in Q3", *The Register*, http://www.theregister.co.uk/2006/11/07/overstock_q3_flop/

2. Ibid.

3. Wailgum, T. (2008, October 30) "Overstock.com's Four-Year ERP Nightmare", CIO Blogs, *CIO.com*, http://blogs.cio.com/thomas_wailgum/overstock_coms_four_year_erp_nightmare

INDEX

Page numbers in *italics* indicate templates.